Rust Programming Language for Cybersecurity

Writing Secure Code to Implementing Advanced Cryptographic Solutions

Jeff Stuart

1

Discover Other Books in the Series

"Rust Programming Language for Beginners: The Ultimate Beginner's Guide to Safe and Fast Programming"

"Rust Programming Language for Operating Systems: Build Secure and High-Performance Operating Systems in Rust"

"Rust Programming language for Network: Build Fast, Secure, and Scalable Systems"

"Rust Programming Language for Web Assembly: Build Blazing-Fast, Next-Gen Web Applications"

"Rust Programming Language for Web Development: Building High-Performance Web Applications and APIs"

"Rust Programming Language for Blockchains: Build Secure, Scalable, and High-Performance Distributed Systems"

"Rust Programming Language for IoT: The Complete Guide to Developing Secure and Efficient Smart Devices"

"Rust programming Language for Artificial Intelligence: High-performance machine learning with unmatched speed, memory safety, and concurrency from AI innovation"

Disclaimer

The information provided in *"**Rust Programming for Cybersecurity: Writing Secure Code to Implementing Advanced Cryptographic Solutions**"* by Jeff Stuart is intended solely for educational and informational purposes.

Introduction

In the current fast-paced digital environment, cybersecurity has become a paramount concern for individuals, organizations, and governments. The rise in cyber threats and vulnerabilities underscores the urgent need to improve our comprehension of secure coding practices. Among the programming languages that provide strong capabilities in this area, Rust is particularly notable for its effectiveness in developing secure, reliable, and high-performance software.

"Rust Programming for Cybersecurity: Writing Secure Code to Implementing Advanced Cryptographic Solutions" aims to be a thorough resource for developers and cybersecurity experts seeking to enhance their understanding of Rust and its relevance in cybersecurity. This book is suitable for both experienced software engineers and those new to programming, offering the essential skills needed to write secure code, implement sophisticated cryptographic solutions, and grasp the intricacies of security in software development.

The text examines the fundamental principles of Rust, highlighting its distinctive features such as ownership, borrowing, and lifetimes, which naturally foster memory safety and concurrency. It will address the significance of secure coding by exploring common vulnerabilities, threat modeling, and best practices that can strengthen applications against cyber threats.

Additionally, the book includes in-depth discussions on the implementation of cryptographic algorithms and protocols using Rust, featuring practical examples that demonstrate how to utilize the language's strengths to develop secure and efficient solutions. Covering a wide range of topics from hashing and encryption to secure communication, this resource is essential for anyone aiming to enhance their cybersecurity expertise..

As technology continues to advance, so too do the tactics employed by cyber adversaries. This ever- changing landscape demands a proactive approach to security, and understanding how to effectively use Rust in building secure applications is a vital step in that direction.

By the end of this book, you will not only gain proficiency in Rust programming but also develop a keen awareness of the critical importance of security in software development. Together, let us embark on this journey towards mastering Rust for cybersecurity and contributing to a safer digital world. Welcome to "Rust Programming for Cybersecurity."

Chapter 1: Getting Started with Rust Programming

Developed by Mozilla Research, it aims to empower developers to create robust and efficient software while preventing common programming errors. With its strong emphasis on memory safety without using garbage collection, Rust has gained significant traction in modern software development.

In this chapter, we will cover the following topics:

What Makes Rust Unique?

Setting Up the Rust Environment

Creating Your First Rust Program

Understanding Rust's Package Manager: Cargo

Basic Syntax and Concepts ### 1. What Makes Rust Unique?

Before diving into code, it's crucial to understand what sets Rust apart from other programming languages:

Memory Safety: Rust uses a system of ownership with a set of rules that the compiler checks at compile time. This prevents data races and guarantees memory safety without a garbage collector.

Concurrency: Rust's ownership model inherently prevents data races at compile time, making concurrent programming more predictable and safe.

Performance: Rust compiles to machine code, which allows for high performance comparable to languages like C and C++. Its zero-cost abstractions ensure that even high-level constructs come with minimal runtime overhead.

Strong Type System: Rust's type system helps catch errors at compile time, reducing the chance of runtime failures.

2. Setting Up the Rust Environment

To start programming in Rust, you'll need to set up your development environment. Follow these steps to get Rust up and running:

Step 1: Install Rust

The easiest way to install Rust is by using `rustup`, a tool that manages Rust versions and associated tools. Open your terminal and run:

```bash
curl --proto '=https' --tlsv1.2 -sSf https://sh.rustup.rs | sh
```

Follow the on-screen instructions to complete the installation. Once it's done, you'll need to adjust your `PATH` environment variable:

```bash
source $HOME/.cargo/env
```

Step 2: Verify Installation

To confirm that Rust is installed correctly, check the version:

```bash
rustc --version
```

```
```

This command should return the installed version of Rust, indicating that everything is set up correctly. ### 3. Creating Your First Rust Program

Now that Rust is installed, let's create a simple "Hello, World!" program: #### Step 1: Create a New Directory

Open your terminal and create a new directory for your project:

```bash
mkdir hello_rust cd hello_rust
```

Step 2: Create a Rust File

Create a new Rust file named `main.rs`:

```bash
touch main.rs
```

Step 3: Write Code

Open the `main.rs` file in your favorite text editor and add the following code:

```rust
fn main() {
println!("Hello, World!");
}
```

Step 4: Compile and Run the Program

To compile and run your program, execute the following commands in your terminal:

```bash
rustc main.rs
./main
```

You should see the output:

```
Hello, World!
```

4. Understanding Rust's Package Manager: Cargo

Rust comes with a built-in package manager and build system called Cargo. Cargo simplifies the process of creating, managing, and distributing Rust projects. Here's how to use it:

Step 1: Create a New Project with Cargo

Instead of manually creating a project structure, you can let Cargo do it for you. Run:

```bash
cargo new hello_cargo cd hello_cargo
```

This creates a new directory named `hello_cargo` with a basic project structure, including a `Cargo.toml` file (for metadata and dependencies) and a `src` directory containing `main.rs`.

Step 2: Build and Run with Cargo

To build and run your newly created Rust program using Cargo, execute:

```bash
cargo run
```

This command compiles the code and runs the resulting binary. You should see the same "Hello, World!" output.

5. Basic Syntax and Concepts

Rust has a unique syntax that combines elements from various programming languages. Here are a few fundamental concepts to understand:

Variables and Mutability: By default, variables in Rust are immutable. You can use the `mut` keyword to make a variable mutable.

```rust
let x = 5; // immutable
let mut y = 10; // mutable y += 5; // now y is 15
```

Data Types: Rust has several built-in data types, including integers, floating-point numbers, booleans, and characters. It also has compound types like tuples and arrays.

Functions: Functions are defined using the `fn` keyword, and they can take parameters and return values.

```rust
fn add(a: i32, b: i32) -> i32 { a + b
```

```
}
```
` ` `

Control Flow: Rust supports standard control flow constructs like `if`, `else`, `loop`, `while`, and `for`.

Congratulations! You've taken your first steps into the world of Rust programming. In this chapter, we covered the unique attributes of Rust, set up the development environment, created a simple program, and explored Cargo. In the upcoming chapters, we will delve deeper into Rust's powerful features, including error handling, ownership, lifetimes, and more.

Installing and Setting Up Rust for Beginners

This chapter aims to guide beginners through the necessary steps to install and set up Rust on their machines, enabling them to embark on their programming journey with confidence.

System Requirements

Before diving into the installation process, it's essential to ensure that your system meets the minimum requirements to run Rust. Rust operates on a variety of platforms, including Windows, macOS, and Linux. Here are the basic requirements:

Operating System: Rust can be installed on Windows 7 and later, macOS 10.7 and later, or most distributions of Linux.

Hardware: A computer with at least 1 GB of RAM

should suffice for basic development. ## Step 1: Installing Rust

The easiest way to install Rust is by using the official tool called `rustup`. This tool manages Rust versions and associated tools, making it easy to keep your installation up to date.

For Windows:

Open the Command Prompt (CMD) or PowerShell.

Download and install `rustup` by entering the following command:
```

curl --proto '=https' --tlsv1.2 -sSf https://sh.rustup.rs | sh
```

Follow the on-screen instructions. You may choose the default installation, which is recommended for beginners.

For macOS/Linux:

Open the Terminal.

Enter the following command to download and install `rustup`:
```

curl --proto '=https' --tlsv1.2 -sSf https://sh.rustup.rs | sh
```

Follow the on-screen prompts to complete the installation.
Post-Installation Steps

After running the installer, you may need to restart your terminal or run the command to configure your shell:

15

```bash
source $HOME/.cargo/env
```

This command adds Rust to your system's PATH, allowing you to use Rust commands from any terminal session.

Step 2: Verifying the Installation

To confirm that Rust has been installed correctly, you should check the version of the Rust compiler (`rustc`). In your terminal, type:

```bash
rustc --version
```

If everything was successful, you should see output similar to:

```
rustc 1.XX.X (abc1234 2023-10-01)
```

The version number will depend on the latest release of Rust. ## Step 3: Setting Up Your Development Environment

Now that you've installed Rust, it's vital to set up a comfortable development environment. Here are some essential tools to consider:

Code Editor

While Rust can be developed using any text editor, using a dedicated code editor or Integrated Development

Environment (IDE) makes the process more efficient. Popular choices include:

Visual Studio Code: Widely used due to its extensive ecosystem of extensions, including those specifically for Rust.

IntelliJ IDEA with the Rust plugin: A robust IDE that offers powerful features like code completion and refactoring.

Rust-specific editors: Tools like "Rust Analyzer" can enhance your coding experience with features like auto-completion, code navigation, and error checking.

Additional Tools

Cargo: Rust's package manager and build system comes bundled with `rustup`. You will use Cargo to manage your Rust projects, libraries, and dependencies.

Verify that Cargo is installed by running:

```bash
cargo --version
```

Rustfmt: A tool to format your Rust code according to style guidelines. Install it using Cargo:

```bash
rustup component add rustfmt
```

Clippy: A linter for Rust that catches common mistakes and improves your code. You can install Clippy with:

```bash

rustup component add clippy

```

Step 4: Writing Your First Rust Program

Now that your environment is set up, it's time to write your first Rust program. Follow these steps:

Create a new project using Cargo:

```bash

cargo new hello_rust cd hello_rust

```

Navigate to the `src` directory and open `main.rs`:

```bash cd src

nano main.rs # or use your preferred text editor

```

Edit `main.rs` to include the following code:

```rust

fn main() { println!("Hello, Rust!");

}

```

Save the file and return to the project root directory.

Compile and run your program with Cargo:

```bash
cargo run
```

You should see the output:

```
Hello, Rust!
```

In the chapters to come, we will dive into data types, functions, control flow, and more, helping you build your skills as a Rust programmer. Happy coding!

Exploring Rust's Syntax and Key Concepts for Security

With its unique approach to memory safety and strong type system, Rust minimizes common programming errors, making it a preferred choice for security-critical applications. In this chapter, we will explore Rust's syntax and core concepts, emphasizing how they contribute to writing secure code.

1. Introduction to Rust Syntax

Rust's syntax is inspired by languages like C, C++, and Python, making it approachable for programmers familiar with these languages. In this section, we will walk through some fundamental aspects of Rust syntax that underline its functionality.

1.1 Variables and Mutability

In Rust, variables are immutable by default. This design

decision encourages developers to think carefully about the state within their applications. For instance:

```rust
let x = 5; // x is immutable
// x = 6; // This would result in a compilation error
```

To declare mutable variables, you must explicitly use the `mut` keyword:

```rust
let mut y = 5;
y += 1; // This is allowed since y is mutable
```

This emphasis on immutability can reduce bugs related to unintended state changes, making it particularly beneficial for security-sensitive applications.

1.2 Data Types and Type Inference

Rust is a statically typed language, meaning the type of every variable is known at compile time. However, it also features type inference, which allows the compiler to deduce types when they are not explicitly provided.

```rust
let a = 10; // i32 inferred
let b: f64 = 10.5; // f64 explicit
```

Strong typing allows developers to catch type-related errors during compilation, rather than at runtime, thereby increasing the robustness of security applications.

1.3 Control Flow

Rust supports standard control flow constructs such as `if`, `while`, and `for`. Here's an example of using an `if` statement:

```rust
let number = 7;
if number < 5 { println!("Less than five!");
} else {
println!("Five or greater!");
}
```

Control flow constructs are essential for implementing logic and conditions that determine the flow of execution in security checks and validations.

2. Core Concepts for Security ### 2.1 Ownership and Borrowing

One of Rust's standout features is its ownership system, which enforces strict rules about how memory is managed. When you create a variable in Rust, you become its owner. When ownership is transferred to another variable, the original variable can no longer be used.

```rust
let s1 = String::from("Hello");
let s2 = s1; // Ownership moved to s2
// println!("{}", s1); // This would cause a compile-time
```

error
```

This concept helps prevent dangling pointers and data races in concurrent programming, which are significant sources of security vulnerabilities.

Borrowing allows functions to temporarily access data without taking ownership. This is done through references, which can be mutable or immutable.

```rust
fn borrow_example(s: &String) { println!("{}", s);

}

let s1 = String::from("Hello"); borrow_example(&s1); // Borrowing s1
```

Rust's borrow checker ensures that there are either multiple immutable references or one mutable reference at any given time, helping to eliminate memory safety issues.

2.2 Pattern Matching

Pattern matching in Rust is a powerful feature that makes it easy to destructure complex data types and handle various cases succinctly. It's often used in `match` statements.

```rust
let number = 3;
```
```

```rust
match number {
1 => println!("One!"),
2 => println!("Two!"),
3 => println!("Three!"),
_ => println!("Not one, two, or three!"),
}
```

Using pattern matching can enhance code security by ensuring that all possible values are accounted for, thus reducing the risk of unexpected behavior.

2.3 Error Handling

Rust implements a robust error handling system via the `Result` and `Option` types. Unlike exceptions in other languages, which can lead to unforeseen states, Rust encourages explicit error handling.

```rust
fn divide(dividend: f64, divisor: f64) -> Result<f64, String> { if divisor == 0.0 {
Err(String::from("Division by zero error!"))
} else {
Ok(dividend / divisor)
}
}
```

By enforcing error handling practices, Rust helps ensure

that security-critical operations fail gracefully rather than leading to undefined behavior, a common attack vector in insecure applications.

3. Concurrency and Safety

Concurrency in Rust is designed to be safe and efficient, minimizing the risk of data races. The language provides mechanisms, such as `Arc` (Atomic Reference Counted) and `Mutex` (Mutual Exclusion), which allow safe shared access to data across threads.

```rust
use std::sync::{Arc, Mutex}; use std::thread;

let data = Arc::new(Mutex::new(0)); let handles: Vec<_> = (0..10).map(|_| {

let data = Arc::clone(&data); thread::spawn(move || {

let mut num = data.lock().unwrap();

*num += 1;

})

}).collect();

for handle in handles { handle.join().unwrap();

}


println!("Result: {}", *data.lock().unwrap());
```

This example illustrates how Rust's concurrency features eliminate vulnerabilities such as race conditions, making concurrent programming safer and more intuitive.

24

By integrating features like ownership, borrowing, and error handling into the language's foundation, Rust provides developers with the tools needed to write safe, concurrent programs. This focus on safety and correctness positions Rust as a strong candidate for developing applications where security is paramount. As we continue to explore Rust's capabilities, we will uncover further nuances that enhance its utility in crafting reliable and secure software.

Chapter 2: Fundamentals of Cybersecurity in Programming

This chapter explores the essential aspects of cybersecurity within the realm of programming, highlighting best practices, principles, and techniques that developers should adopt to enhance the security of their software.

2.1 Comprehending Cyber Threats

Prior to implementing defensive strategies, it is vital to understand the various types of threats that can exploit weaknesses in code. Cyber threats can be classified into several categories:

2.1.1 Malware

Malware, which encompasses viruses, worms, and Trojan horses, infiltrates systems with the intent to cause damage. It is imperative for programmers to ensure that their applications are safeguarded against code injections that may result in malware infections.

2.1.2 Phishing Attacks

Phishing entails deceiving users into divulging sensitive information by posing as a legitimate entity. Developers should take steps to educate users and integrate verification protocols to combat these types of attacks.

2.1.3 Denial of Service (DoS) Attacks

These attacks render services inaccessible by inundating them with excessive traffic. It is essential for developers to understand how to create resilient applications capable of mitigating the effects of DoS attacks.### 2.1.4 SQL

Injection

SQL injection is a common attack where malicious SQL statements are inserted into an entry field for execution. This can compromise databases and expose sensitive information, demonstrating the critical need for secure coding practices.

2.1.5 Cross-Site Scripting (XSS)

XSS attacks occur when an attacker injects malicious scripts into trusted web applications, enabling the execution of arbitrary scripts in a user's browser. Preventing XSS requires understanding how to properly escape and sanitize user input.

2.2 Secure Coding Practices

Implementing secure coding practices is fundamental for protecting applications from various vulnerabilities. Below are key principles that programmers should adhere to:

2.2.1 Input Validation

One of the first lines of defense in programming is validating user input. Ensuring that data conforms to expected formats can prevent numerous attacks, including SQL injection and XSS. Implement allow-lists where feasible, accepting only inputs that meet specific criteria.

2.2.2 Principle of Least Privilege

The principle of least privilege dictates that users and processes should only have the necessary permissions to perform their functions. This minimizes potential damage from a security breach. Developers can enforce this principle by managing permissions judiciously in their applications.

2.2.3 Error Handling

Error messages, if not properly managed, can reveal sensitive information about an application's infrastructure. Programmers should ensure that error messages do not disclose details that could be exploited by attackers. Instead, implement generic error responses while logging detailed errors for internal review.

2.2.4 Encryption

Data encryption is essential for protecting sensitive information, both at rest and in transit. Programmers should use strong encryption standards (such as AES) and secure protocols (like HTTPS) to ensure data confidentiality and integrity.

2.2.5 Regular Updates and Patch Management

Software vulnerabilities are regularly discovered, and failing to update code can expose applications to attacks. Developers should prioritize regular updates, applying patches consistently to mitigate risks.

2.3 Threat Modeling

Threat modeling is a proactive approach that helps developers anticipate potential threats and vulnerabilities in their software. This process typically follows these steps:

Identify Assets: Determine what sensitive data or components are critical to the application.

Identify Threat Agents: Recognize who might want to exploit vulnerabilities and what their motivations could be, including hackers, competitors, or state actors.

Identify Vulnerabilities: Analyze potential weaknesses

in the application that could be exploited.

Develop Mitigation Strategies: Establish countermeasures based on the identified threats and vulnerabilities.

2.4 Security Testing

Security testing is an integral part of the software development lifecycle (SDLC). Various techniques can be employed, including:

2.4.1 Static Code Analysis

Tools can analyze code without executing it to identify flaws, vulnerabilities, and deviations from secure coding standards. Regular static analysis should be part of the development process.

2.4.2 Dynamic Analysis

This method involves running applications in real-time to identify security vulnerabilities. Techniques such as penetration testing can reveal weaknesses that static analysis might miss.

2.4.3 Code Reviews

Conducting regular peer reviews of code can help in identifying security issues early in the development process. Encouraging a culture of shared responsibility for security in programming teams is beneficial.

2.5 The Role of Education and Awareness

Ultimately, even the best practices are only as effective as the people implementing them. Cultivating a culture of cybersecurity awareness among developers is fundamental. Continuous education through training sessions, workshops, and resources can keep programmers informed about the latest threats and security practices.

2.5.1 Certification and Training

Investing in professional certification programs, such as Certified Ethical Hacker (CEH) or Certified Information Systems Security Professional (CISSP), can empower developers with the knowledge necessary to build secure software.

2.5.2 Knowledge Sharing

Encouraging teams to share knowledge through internal forums or code-sharing platforms enhances collective intelligence around security practices and helps forge a robust security-first mindset.

By embracing these fundamentals of cybersecurity in programming, we can ensure that innovations are not only effective but also secure. In the next chapter, we will explore the emerging technologies in cybersecurity and how they can be integrated into programming practices to enhance security measures further.

Understanding Cyber Threats and Attack Vectors

In the rapidly evolving landscape of technology, understanding cybersecurity threats is crucial for developers, especially when programming languages like Rust are increasingly adopted for their performance, safety, and concurrency features. This chapter delves into the key cyber threats and attack vectors that may affect applications built with Rust, providing developers with the knowledge they need to design secure systems.

1. Overview of Cybersecurity Risks

Every software application, regardless of the programming language used, is susceptible to various cyber threats. These threats can be classified into several categories, including:

Malware: Malicious software designed to harm, exploit, or disable systems.

Phishing: Deceptive attempts to obtain sensitive information, often through social engineering tactics.

Denial-of-Service (DoS): Attacks that aim to render services unavailable by overwhelming them with traffic.

SQL Injection: A technique where attackers manipulate SQL statements to gain unauthorized access or alter data.

While Rust's unique features can mitigate some risks, it's essential to recognize that no language is immune to threats. Understanding how these risks manifest within the Rust ecosystem is the first step toward developing secure applications.

2. Rust-Specific Threats and Vulnerabilities

Rust is designed with safety in mind, particularly regarding memory management. However, certain vulnerabilities can still arise in Rust applications:

2.1 Improper Error Handling

Rust encourages the use of `Result` and `Option` types to handle potential errors. However, if developers neglect proper error handling, they can inadvertently introduce vulnerabilities, such as:

Information Leakage: Returning detailed error messages can expose system internals to potential attackers.

Uncaught Panics: Failing to manage panic scenarios can lead to denial-of-service conditions where the application crashes unexpectedly.

2.2 Unsafe Code

While Rust segregates safe and unsafe code, developers sometimes need to use `unsafe` blocks for performance or interoperability purposes. This introduces risks, such as:

Memory Safety Issues: Using pointers incorrectly can lead to null pointer dereferencing, buffer overflows, or use-after-free vulnerabilities.

Data Races: Concurrent access to shared mutable data can lead to unpredictable behaviors, potentially exploited by malicious actors.

2.3 Dependency Vulnerabilities

Most Rust applications rely on third-party libraries, integrated through Cargo. Vulnerabilities can arise from:

Outdated Dependencies: Using deprecated libraries can expose applications to known vulnerabilities.

Supply Chain Attacks: Compromised packages in the Rust ecosystem can introduce malicious code into otherwise secure applications.

3. Common Attack Vectors in Rust Applications

Understanding attack vectors is essential to safeguarding

applications. Here are some common attack vectors relevant to Rust:

3.1 Code Injection Attacks

While Rust's strict typing and ownership model can mitigate some injection vulnerabilities, developers must still be vigilant against:

Command Injection: If user input is improperly sanitized before being passed to system commands or APIs, attackers could execute arbitrary code.

3.2 Cross-Site Scripting (XSS)

When building web applications using frameworks like Rocket or Actix, developers must be cautious of XSS vulnerabilities. Improper output encoding can allow attackers to inject scripts that execute in the user's browser.

3.3 Insecure Deserialization

When deserializing data (often from JSON), if input is not validated, there's a risk of deserialization attacks. Attackers may craft payloads that exploit weaknesses, leading to arbitrary code execution.

3.4 Man-in-the-Middle (MitM) Attacks

Network communications in Rust applications can be intercepted if protocols are not implemented securely. Always use TLS/SSL to ensure data integrity and confidentiality.

4. Best Practices for Secure Rust Programming

To bolster security in Rust applications, developers should adhere to the following best practices: ### 4.1 Leverage

Rust's Safety Features

Utilize Rust's strong type system, ownership model, and borrow checker to enforce memory safety and concurrency. Always prefer safe APIs and eliminate the use of `unsafe` code wherever possible.

4.2 Regular Dependency Audits

Utilize tools like `cargo audit` and `cargo tree` to identify outdated or vulnerable dependencies. Regularly check for updates and consider the stability and reputation of external libraries.

4.3 Input Validation and Sanitization

Always validate and sanitize user inputs. Use libraries that provide tools for secure parsing and escaping, particularly in web applications, to prevent injection attacks.

4.4 Implement Robust Error Handling

Develop a clear error management strategy that prioritizes security. Avoid exposing sensitive error messages and employ logging solutions that capture necessary details without disclosing vulnerabilities.

4.5 Educate and Train Development Teams

Continuous training on secure coding practices, awareness of current threats, and effective response strategies can empower development teams to better secure Rust applications.

By embracing Rust's safety features and adhering to best practices in security, developers can build resilient applications capable of withstanding the evolving landscape of cyber threats. Continual vigilance, education, and adaptation to newly emerging risks will enhance the security posture of Rust-based systems, fostering a safer digital environment.

Cybersecurity Principles: Confidentiality, Integrity, and Availability (CIA)

Central to this field are three foundational principles: Confidentiality, Integrity, and Availability, often abbreviated as CIA. These principles form the bedrock of effective cybersecurity strategies and serve as guiding tenets for protecting information systems and data from unauthorized access, corruption, and disruptions.

Confidentiality

Confidentiality refers to the protection of sensitive information from unauthorized access and disclosure. It ensures that data, whether it is personal, financial, or proprietary, is only accessible to those who have the requisite permissions to view it. Breaches of confidentiality can lead to significant risks, including financial loss, reputational damage, and legal consequences.

Mechanisms of Confidentiality

To uphold confidentiality, organizations implement various safeguards, including:

Access Controls: Systems are restricted through user authentication methods such as passwords, biometrics, and multi-factor authentication (MFA) to prevent unauthorized access.

Encryption: Encrypting sensitive data, whether at rest (stored) or in transit (being transmitted), ensures that even if unauthorized individuals gain access to it, they cannot decipher it without the appropriate decryption keys.

Data Masking: In environments where data is used for testing or development, masking techniques ensure that sensitive information is obscured.

User Awareness Training: Employees are educated about the importance of confidentiality and trained to recognize phishing attempts and social engineering tactics that target sensitive information.

Challenges to Confidentiality

Despite robust measures, challenges persist in maintaining confidentiality. Human error, such as inadvertently sharing information with the wrong recipient, and sophisticated cyberattacks, including ransomware and insider threats, can undermine confidentiality efforts. It is vital for organizations to continuously evaluate and evolve their strategies to address these risks.

Integrity

Integrity ensures the accuracy and consistency of data over its lifecycle. When information is corrupted, whether accidentally or maliciously, its reliability is compromised. Maintaining integrity means that data remains trustworthy and can be relied upon for decision-making processes, audits, and reporting.

Mechanisms of Integrity

Various methods can be employed to preserve data

integrity:

Hashing: Creating a unique hash value for data allows for its integrity to be verified. Any alteration in the data results in a different hash, signaling potential tampering.

Access Controls: Similar to confidentiality, integrity is supported by restricting access. Limiting who can modify data reduces the risk of unauthorized changes.

Audit Trails: Implementing logging and monitoring mechanisms helps track changes to data and can provide insights for forensic analysis in the event of a breach.

Version Control: For collaborative environments, maintaining version histories of documents can help revert changes if data is modified and needs to be restored to a previous state.

Challenges to Integrity

Integrity is often challenged by data corruption due to hardware failures, software bugs, or cyberattacks like man-in-the-middle attacks. Organizations must adopt a proactive approach, conducting regular data integrity checks and employing redundancy strategies to mitigate such risks.

Availability

Availability ensures that information and resources are accessible to authorized users when needed. A breach of availability can lead to business disruptions, loss of productivity, and negative impacts on customer trust.

Mechanisms of Availability

To maintain availability, organizations implement several strategies:

Redundancy: Having backup systems, data replication, and redundant servers can mitigate the impact of hardware failures or cyberattacks aimed at disrupting services.

Load Balancing: Distributing traffic across multiple servers can help prevent overload and ensure consistent access to services.

Regular Maintenance: Conducting routine maintenance on systems and infrastructure helps identify vulnerabilities before they can be exploited.

Incident Response Planning: Preparing an incident response plan ensures that organizations can quickly address issues that threaten availability, such as DDoS attacks or natural disasters.

Challenges to Availability

Ensuring availability presents unique challenges, including denial-of-service (DoS) attacks, system failures, and natural disasters. Organizations must remain agile, capable of responding effectively to such incidents to restore normal operations swiftly.

The Interconnectedness of CIA

While confidentiality, integrity, and availability are distinct principles, they are deeply interconnected. A breach of one can compromise the others. For instance, if an attacker compromises the integrity of a system, the associated data may not only become unreliable but could also lead to unauthorized access, thereby impacting confidentiality. Conversely, an availability issue could hinder access to critical systems, affecting the integrity of transactions and decision-making. Therefore, a holistic approach considering all three aspects is essential for comprehensive cybersecurity.

Confidentiality, integrity, and availability are the cornerstones of cybersecurity. By understanding and prioritizing these principles, organizations can better protect their information assets and mitigate risks associated with cyber threats. In a landscape characterized by rapid technological advancements and evolving threats, a robust commitment to the CIA triad will enable organizations to navigate challenges and secure their digital environments effectively.

Chapter 3: Rust's Unique Features for Secure Programming

This chapter delves into the unique features of Rust that make it exceptionally suited for developing secure applications, tackling common programming pitfalls head-on.

3.1 Memory Safety Without Garbage Collection

One of Rust's cornerstone features is its strict approach to memory safety. Traditional languages like C and C++ provide developers with great control over memory management but leave them vulnerable to a range of issues such as buffer overflows, use-after-free errors, and memory leaks. Rust circumvents these vulnerabilities through a concept known as ownership.

3.1.1 Ownership System

Rust's ownership model revolves around three main principles: ownership, borrowing, and lifetimes. When a variable is assigned a value, it becomes the owner of that value. At any given time, a value can have only one owner. When the owner goes out of scope, Rust automatically deallocates the value, preventing memory leaks and use-after-free errors.

Borrowing allows developers to temporarily access a value without taking ownership. Rust enforces strict rules on borrowing, ensuring that either multiple immutable references or one mutable reference can exist at a time. This prevents data races at compile time, a common source of security vulnerabilities.

3.1.2 Lifetimes

Lifetimes are another crucial aspect of Rust's memory safety guarantees. They define how long references to values can be valid. By utilizing lifetimes, Rust helps developers track the scope of references and ensures that they do not outlive the data they point to. This feature minimizes the potential for dangling pointers, a prevalent source of memory-related bugs.

3.2 Concurrency and Thread Safety

Concurrency is a double-edged sword in programming; it can improve performance but also lead to hard-to-diagnose bugs if not managed correctly. Rust's approach to concurrency minimizes the chance of deadlocks and race conditions while maximizing efficiency.

3.2.1 Fearless Concurrency

Rust introduces the concept of "fearless concurrency." By leveraging the ownership and type systems, Rust ensures that many concurrency errors are caught at compile time. For instance, when multiple threads attempt to access shared data, Rust enforces rules that prevent mutable data from being accessed simultaneously, eliminating data races.

3.2.2 The `Send` and `Sync` Traits

Rust features two key traits, `Send` and `Sync`, that help manage concurrency. A type is `Send` if it can be transferred across thread boundaries, while a type is `Sync` if it can be safely referenced from multiple threads. These traits enable the compiler to enforce safe concurrency patterns, allowing developers to build multi-threaded applications confidently.

3.3 Error Handling and Result Types

Insecure programming often arises from improper error handling. Rust places a strong emphasis on handling errors explicitly, reducing the likelihood of unchecked exceptions leading to vulnerabilities.

3.3.1 The `Result` and `Option` Types

Rust introduces the `Result` and `Option` types as robust mechanisms for error handling. The `Result` type represents either a success or an error, requiring developers to handle both cases explicitly. This design encourages thorough error checking and propagation, reducing the chances of overlooking critical failures.

The `Option` type encapsulates values that may be absent, providing a clear and safe way to represent optional data without resorting to null references, which have historically been a source of vulnerabilities in other languages.

3.4 Strong Type System and Pattern Matching

A strong, statically typed language can prevent a multitude of errors, and Rust's type system is both expressive and stringent. It enables developers to catch type-related errors at compile-time rather than at runtime.

3.4.1 Algebraic Data Types

Rust supports algebraic data types, allowing developers to create complex data structures while maintaining type safety. This feature, when combined with pattern matching, empowers developers to write exhaustive and clear code that handles every possible scenario. By forcing developers to consider all possible cases, Rust reduces the likelihood of unhandled exceptions.

3.4.2 Immutability by Default

Immutability is another vital feature in Rust. Variables are immutable by default, promoting a functional programming style that discourages side effects. This practice leads to more predictable code and reduces the risk of unintended mutations that can compromise security.

3.5 Ecosystem and Community Focused on Security

Beyond the language's features, Rust's ecosystem and community are dedicated to enhancing secure programming practices.

3.5.1 Crates and Libraries

The Rust ecosystem boasts a rich collection of libraries, known as crates, which prioritize secure development. The Rust community actively reviews and maintains these libraries, promoting tools and practices that minimize vulnerabilities.

3.5.2 Documentation and Learning Resources

Comprehensive documentation and educational resources are abundant in the Rust community. Developers new to Rust are encouraged to learn best practices from the outset, fostering a culture of security-minded programming.

Rust's unique features form a solid foundation for secure programming, addressing many of the common pitfalls that plague other languages. Its ownership model, strong concurrency guarantees, explicit error handling, and emphasis on immutability contribute to a safer and more predictable programming experience.

Ownership, Borrowing, and Lifetimes for Preventing Memory Errors

This can lead to common pitfalls such as dangling pointers, buffer overflows, and memory leaks. Rust, a systems programming language designed for safety and concurrency, introduces a unique approach to memory management through the concepts of ownership, borrowing, and lifetimes. This chapter will explore these concepts in-depth, illustrating how they work together to prevent memory errors and ensure safe coding practices.

1. Ownership

At the heart of Rust's memory management system is the concept of ownership. In Rust, every value has a single owner, which is the variable that holds that value. When ownership of a value is transferred (or moved) to another variable, the original variable can no longer access that value.

1.1 The Ownership Rules

Rust's ownership model is governed by a few fundamental rules:

Each value in Rust has a variable that is its **owner**.

A value can have only one owner at a time.

When the owner of a value goes out of scope, Rust automatically deallocates that value.

These rules help Rust manage memory automatically, preventing memory leaks and ensuring that memory is freed when it is no longer needed.

1.2 Move Semantics

When a variable is assigned to another variable, it may result in a move rather than a copy. For instance:

```rust
let s1 = String::from("Hello, Rust!"); let s2 = s1; // Move occurs

// println!("{}", s1); // Error: s1 has been moved
```

In the example above, `s1` no longer has ownership of the string once it is assigned to `s2`. This prevents accidental duplication and ensures only one owner exists at a time.

2. Borrowing

While ownership guarantees memory safety, it can also create limitations, particularly regarding sharing data between different parts of a program. Rust addresses this challenge with **borrowing**, which allows you to hold references to values without taking ownership.

2.1 References

In Rust, references are denoted by the `&` symbol. Borrowing comes in two forms: mutable and immutable.

Immutable Borrowing: You can borrow a value immutably when you only need read access. Multiple immutable borrows are allowed simultaneously.

```rust
fn main() {
```

```rust
    let s = String::from("Hello, World!");

    let r1 = &s; // Immutable borrow
    let r2 = &s; // Another immutable borrow
    println!("Borrowed: {}, {}", r1, r2);
}
```

Mutable Borrowing: When you need to modify a value, you can borrow it mutably using `&mut`. However, only one mutable borrow is allowed at a time, which prevents data races.

```rust
fn main() {
    let mut s = String::from("Hello");
    let r_mut = &mut s; // Mutable borrow
    r_mut.push_str(", Rust!"); // Modifying the borrowed value
    println!("Modified: {}", r_mut);
}
```

2.2 Borrowing Rules

Rust's borrowing system adheres to strict rules:

You can have either one mutable reference or any number of immutable references to a piece of data, but not both at the same time.

References must always be valid, meaning they cannot outlive the data they point to.

These rules ensure that borrowing does not introduce memory errors typical in languages with less stringent memory management feature.

3. Lifetimes

While ownership and borrowing create the foundation for memory safety in Rust, lifetimes further refine how references are validated. A lifetime is a construct that denotes the scope for which a reference is valid. Rust uses lifetimes to ensure that references do not outlive the data they refer to, thereby preventing dangling references.

3.1 Lifetime Annotations

In more complex scenarios, you may need to explicitly annotate lifetimes. This is done using the syntax

`<'a>`, where `'a` represents a specific lifetime.

Consider a function that returns the longer of two string slices:

```rust
fn longest<'a>(s1: &'a str, s2: &'a str) -> &'a str {

if s1.len() > s2.len(){ s1
} else { s2
}
}
```

In this example, the function guarantees that the returned reference will live at least as long as the shorter input string reference, effectively preventing dangling references and ensuring safety.

3.2 Lifetime Elision

To simplify function signatures, Rust employs lifetime elision rules that allow the compiler to infer lifetimes in certain contexts, reducing verbosity and improving readability.

By enforcing strict ownership rules and providing safe borrowing mechanisms, Rust allows developers to write high-performance code while enhancing safety and reducing the likelihood of bugs. Understanding and utilizing these concepts is essential for any developer looking to leverage the power and safety that Rust offers in systems programming.

Rust's Safety Features: Type System and Error Handling

This chapter explores the intricacies of Rust's safety features, emphasizing how its type system and error handling contribute to safer code and enhanced developer productivity.

The Type System

Strongly Typed Language

Rust is a strongly typed language, which means that every variable's type is known at compile time. This design choice allows for several benefits:

Early Error Detection: Syntax and type errors are caught early in the development process, reducing the likelihood of runtime failures.

Optimization Opportunities: The compiler can optimize code more effectively when it understands the data types involved.

Ownership and Borrowing

One of Rust's most revolutionary concepts is its ownership model, which governs how memory is managed without a garbage collector. The core principles include:

Ownership: Each value in Rust has a single owner, and when the owner goes out of scope, the value is dropped. This prevents memory leaks and ensures that resources are automatically deallocated.

Borrowing: Values can be borrowed either immutably or mutably. Immutable borrows allow multiple references to a value, while a mutable borrow grants exclusive access. This guarantees data race freedom at compile time, preventing concurrent access issues.

These ownership and borrowing rules ensure that references do not outlive the data they point to, addressing a common source of bugs in other languages.

Lifetimes

To manage the scope of references, Rust introduces the concept of lifetimes. Lifetimes are annotations that help the Rust compiler track how long references are valid. This prevents dangling references — a frequent issue in languages without such strict guarantees. By enforcing clear lifetime rules, Rust allows developers to write safer concurrent code that is immune to potential vulnerabilities.

Error Handling

Compile-Time Safety

Rust distinguishes between different kinds of errors through its type system, specifically through the `Result` and `Option` types. By requiring developers to handle potential errors explicitly, Rust avoids many pitfalls associated with exception-based error handling found in other languages.

Result Type

The `Result` type is an enum that encapsulates outcome states, typically representing the success or failure of operations:

```rust
enum Result<T, E> {

Ok(T),        // Indicates success and contains a value of type T. Err(E),        // Indicates failure and contains an error of type E.

}
```

When using functions that return a `Result`, developers are compelled to handle both outcomes, promoting a conscious approach to error management.

Example of a function returning a `Result`:

```rust
fn divide(numerator: f64, denominator: f64) ->
Result<f64, String> { if denominator == 0.0 {

Err(String::from("Division by zero"))

} else {

Ok(numerator / denominator)

}

}
```

When calling this function, the caller must deal with the potential for failure:

```rust
match divide(10.0, 0.0) {

Ok(result) => println!("Result: {}", result), Err(e) =>
println!("Error: {}", e),

}
```

This pattern ensures robustness and clarity, as each possible failure must be addressed. #### Option Type

Similar to `Result`, the `Option` type is used when a value may or may not be present. It also prevents null-pointer dereferencing, a notorious issue in languages with null values.

```rust
enum Option<T> {
```

```
Some(T), // Contains a value of type T None,    //
Represents the absence of a value

}
```
` ` `

Panic Handling

In Rust, a situation that leads to a panic usually indicates a bug in the program. While Rust encourages safe error handling through `Result` and `Option`, it also allows for panicking when the program encounters an unexpected state. However, panics are treated as unrecoverable errors and should be used judiciously. By maintaining clear boundaries between recoverable and unrecoverable errors, Rust keeps the codebase clean and predictable.

Practical Implications

Rust's safety features foster a development environment that minimizes common programming errors, leading to more reliable software. By forcing developers to confront potential issues directly, Rust enables a mindset focused on rigorous error handling and resource management. Consequently, this reduces runtime bugs and improves overall code quality.

Testing and Documentation

Rust's type system and error handling mechanisms simplify testing and documentation. With explicit types and well-defined error handling paths, it is easier to write tests that assert expected behaviors and error conditions. Furthermore, Rust's documentation tools automatically generate documentation that includes information about function return types and potential errors, streamlining the onboarding of new developers.

By prioritizing compile-time safety, ownership, and explicit error handling, Rust not only helps developers write secure code but also fosters a culture of careful resource management and error awareness. As software systems become increasingly complex, Rust offers a compelling alternative to traditional languages, ensuring that safety, performance, and concurrency can coexist harmoniously.

Chapter 4: Writing Secure Code in Rust

This chapter will explore Rust's safety features, best practices for writing secure code, and common pitfalls to avoid, making it a valuable resource for developers and security professionals alike.

The Foundations of Rust's Security ### 1. Memory Safety

At the heart of Rust's design philosophy is memory safety. Rust eliminates common programming errors that lead to security vulnerabilities, such as buffer overflows, null pointer dereferences, and data races. This is achieved through its ownership model, which enforces strict borrowing and lifetimes at compile time.

Understanding these concepts is fundamental to writing secure Rust code.

Ownership and Borrowing

Rust's ownership model ensures that each piece of data has a single owner, and when that owner goes out of scope, the data is automatically deallocated. Borrowing (both mutable and immutable) allows for references to data without taking ownership, but the compiler enforces rules that prevent data races. This prevents vulnerabilities that can arise from concurrent data access, which are often exploited by attackers.

2. Safe and Unsafe Code

While Rust promotes safety, it also provides an "unsafe" keyword that allows developers to perform operations that bypass the compiler's safety checks. This is useful for interfacing with low-level system components or for high-performance code, but it comes with increased responsibility.

When to Use Unsafe Code

It's vital to use unsafe code sparingly and with caution. Always question whether unsafe operations are necessary, and document their usage meticulously to prevent introducing vulnerabilities. When engaging with unsafe code, you should:

Ensure that all invariants are maintained.

Avoid exposing unsafe abstractions to other parts of your code base.

Use thorough testing and code reviews.

Best Practices for Writing Secure Code in Rust ### 1. Leverage Rust's Type System

Rust's type system serves as a powerful tool to enforce correctness and security. Use strong type definitions to model your domain accurately and leverage enums for representing states. This practice helps prevent logic errors and mitigates risks related to improper data handling.

2. Validate and Sanitize Input

Just like in any programming language, accepting user input without validation can lead to injection vulnerabilities and other security issues. Always validate and sanitize input data at the boundaries of your application.

Example:

```rust
```

```
fn validate_username(username: &str) -> Result<(),
String> { if username.len() < 3 || username.len() > 20 {

return Err("Username must be between 3 and 20
characters.".to_string());

} Ok(())

}
```
` ` `

3. Use Error Handling Wisely

Rust's proper error handling using `Result` and `Option` types encourages developers to explicitly manage failure states. Avoid using panic in production code, as it can expose sensitive information and lead to denial of service.

4. Minimize the Use of Unsafe Code

As previously discussed, unsafe code must be minimized. If you find yourself needing unsafe blocks, consider splitting the unsafe logic from the safe API and ensuring that thorough testing is applied.

5. Apply Principle of Least Privilege

When designing features that interact with system resources, always operate with the least privilege necessary. This minimizes the impact of potential vulnerabilities, limiting an attacker's access to sensitive resources.

6. Keep Your Dependencies Secure

Third-party libraries can introduce vulnerabilities. Utilize `cargo audit` to check for known vulnerabilities, and stay informed about updates for the libraries you depend on. Auditing your dependency tree is crucial for maintaining a secure application.

7. Enforce Secure Coding Practices

Institute coding standards that encourage secure coding practices. Conduct regular code reviews with a focus on security, and foster a culture of security awareness among developers.

Common Pitfalls to Avoid

1. Ignoring Compiler Warnings

Rust's compiler provides invaluable warnings that serve as guidelines for writing safe and secure code. Ignoring these warnings can lead to overlooked issues. Always compile with warnings enabled and address them appropriately.

2. Misunderstanding Lifetimes

While Rust's lifetime system is a powerful feature, it can be complex and easily misunderstood. Failing to grasp how lifetimes work can result in erroneous memory access patterns and vulnerabilities. Take the time to understand lifetimes fully.

3. Neglecting Concurrency Safety

Concurrent programming is inherently challenging. Rust's safety features help, but understanding synchronization mechanisms is essential to avoid introducing data races. Always employ Mutexes or similar synchronization primitives when accessing shared resources.

4. Failing to Keep Security In Mind Throughout the Development Cycle

Security should not be an afterthought. Implement secure coding practices from the outset, and prioritize security throughout the entire development and deployment lifecycle of your application.

Writing secure code in Rust involves understanding and leveraging the language's powerful guarantees around memory safety, fostering a mindset of vigilance regarding input validation, proper error handling, and minimizing the reliance on unsafe code. By following best practices, being aware of common pitfalls, and fostering a culture of security, developers can harness Rust's capabilities to create robust, safe applications capable of resisting a multitude of security threats.

Secure Coding Standards and Best Practices in Rust

This chapter will explore secure coding standards and best practices in Rust to help developers write robust and secure code.

Understanding the Rust Safety Guarantees

At the core of Rust's appeal is its commitment to memory safety without a garbage collector. Rust's ownership model, borrowing rules, and data types are designed to prevent common programming errors that lead to vulnerabilities. Understanding these guarantees is the first step toward writing secure Rust code.

Ownership and Borrowing

Rust's ownership system ensures that every piece of data has a single owner at any time. Borrowing allows references to be created temporarily without transferring ownership. The Rust compiler enforces strict rules on ownership and lifetimes, preventing issues like double frees, dangling pointers, and data races at compile time rather than runtime.

Immutability by Default

In Rust, variables are immutable by default. This design choice reduces the likelihood of unintended state changes, which can lead to vulnerabilities. Developers should leverage immutability wherever possible, making it clear when mutations are necessary.

Secure Coding Best Practices

1. Use Built-in Types and Structures

Rust provides a rich set of built-in types and data structures that are designed with safety in mind. Instead of using primitive types, developers should prefer higher-level constructs like `Option`, `Result`, and collections from the standard library, which incorporate safety checks inherently.

2. Proper Error Handling

Rust encourages robust error handling through the use of the `Result` and `Option` types. Instead of panicking or silently ignoring errors, developers should handle potential errors gracefully. This ensures that the application behaves predictably and securely, even in unexpected situations.

```rust
```

```
fn  read_file(file_path:  &str)  ->  Result<String,
std::io::Error>  {  let  content  =
std::fs::read_to_string(file_path)?;
```

Ok(content)

}

` ` `

3. Validate Input

Always validate input data before processing it. Whether reading from files, receiving network requests, or accepting user input, ensuring that data adheres to expected types and formats is crucial for preventing attacks such as injection and buffer overflows. Rust's strong type system allows for thorough validation of inputs.

4. Avoid Unsafe Code

Rust provides an `unsafe` keyword that allows developers to opt out of certain safety guarantees. While there are legitimate use cases for using unsafe code, it introduces potential vulnerabilities if not handled correctly. Developers should restrict its use and thoroughly document why it is necessary.

5. Leverage Libraries and Crates

The Rust ecosystem includes many libraries and crates that are actively maintained and vetted by the community. Leveraging these resources can save time, reduce the likelihood of introducing bugs, and ensure that best practices are followed. Always review the security practices of third-party libraries and choose those with good reputations.

6. Keep Dependencies Updated

Regularly updating dependencies is crucial to maintain security. The Rust package manager, Cargo, simplifies the process of managing and updating dependencies. Use tools like `cargo audit` and `cargo geiger` to identify vulnerabilities in the dependencies and track their usage in the codebase.

7. Understand Concurrency

Concurrency can introduce complex issues like data races and deadlocks if not managed correctly. Rust's ownership model helps mitigate these issues, but developers should remain vigilant about how they share data across threads. Using synchronization primitives such as `Mutex` and `RwLock` as needed can help maintain data integrity.

8. Write Tests

Unit tests and integration tests are essential for verifying that code behaves as expected. In Rust, adding tests is straightforward and encouraged. Writing tests that account for edge cases and potential failure scenarios can help uncover vulnerabilities early in the development process.

```rust
#[cfg(test)] mod tests {

use super::*;

#[test]

fn test_read_file_valid() {

let result = read_file("valid/path/to/file.txt");
assert!(result.is_ok());

}
```

```
#[test]
fn test_read_file_invalid() {
let    result    =    read_file("invalid/path/to/file.txt");
assert!(result.is_err());
}
}
```
```

### 9. Use Logging and Monitoring

Implement logging to detect and respond to security incidents. Rust's ecosystem includes libraries like `log` which can help developers log various levels of information. Ensure that logs do not expose sensitive information, and consider integrating monitoring solutions to detect unusual patterns in application behavior.

By understanding Rust's safety guarantees, writing clear and maintainable code, properly managing errors and inputs, and using community-supported libraries, developers can significantly reduce the risk of vulnerabilities in their applications. As Rust continues to evolve, staying informed about the latest best practices and tools will be crucial to maintaining robust security in software development.
```

Avoiding Common Vulnerabilities: Buffer Overflows, Null Pointers, and Race Conditions

Among the myriad of vulnerabilities that can plague software systems, buffer overflows, null pointers, and race conditions are some of the most common and pervasive issues. This chapter aims to explore these vulnerabilities, their potential impact, and effective strategies for avoiding them.

Buffer Overflows

Understanding Buffer Overflows

A buffer overflow occurs when a program writes more data to a buffer than it can hold, resulting in adjacent memory locations being overwritten. This can lead to unexpected behavior, crashing the program, or allowing an attacker to execute arbitrary code. Buffer overflows are particularly dangerous in languages like C and C++ where boundary checking is not enforced automatically.

Consequences of Buffer Overflows

The consequences of buffer overflows can be severe. Attackers often exploit these vulnerabilities to gain control over a system, execute malicious code, or escalate privileges. For instance, in 2003, the Blaster Worm exploited a buffer overflow in Microsoft's DCOM service, leading to widespread disruptions.

Prevention Strategies

To avoid buffer overflows, developers can adopt several best practices:

Use Safe Functions: Prefer functions that perform boundary checks, such as `strncpy` over `strcpy`, and `snprintf` over `sprintf`. These functions limit the number of bytes written to a buffer.

Bounds Checking: Implement checks to ensure that data written to buffers does not exceed their allocated size. Validating input sizes and types helps mitigate risks.

Static Analysis Tools: Utilize static analysis tools to identify potential buffer overflow vulnerabilities during the development process. These tools can analyze code for common patterns that may lead to overflows.

Memory Management: Use high-level programming languages like Java or Python which manage memory automatically, reducing the risk of overflow vulnerabilities inherent in manual memory management.

Null Pointers

Understanding Null Pointers

Null pointer dereferencing occurs when a program attempts to access or modify the data at a memory location referenced by a null pointer (a pointer that does not point to a valid address). This often leads to segmentation faults or program crashes, making systems unresponsive.

Consequences of Null Pointer Dereferencing

When null pointers are dereferenced, the impact can vary from crashes to denial of service attacks. For example, a web server that crashes due to a null pointer dereference might expose users to temporary unavailability of a service, potentially leading to loss of revenue and trust.

Prevention Strategies

To mitigate issues related to null pointers:

Initialize Pointers: Always initialize pointers to a valid memory address or to null when they are declared. This practice helps avoid undefined behavior.

Null Checks: Implement rigorous null checks before dereferencing pointers. Code should verify that pointers are not null before any operation is performed on them.

Use Smart Pointers: In C++, utilize smart pointers (like `std::shared_ptr` or `std::unique_ptr`). These classes manage memory automatically and help prevent dereferencing of null pointers.

Code Review and Testing: Conduct thorough code reviews and implement unit testing to identify potential issues related to null pointer dereferencing early in the development cycle.

Race Conditions

Understanding Race Conditions

A race condition occurs when the outcome of a process depends on the sequence or timing of uncontrollable events, such as the completion of threads. When multiple threads access shared resources without proper synchronization, they can lead to inconsistent or corrupted data states.

Consequences of Race Conditions

Race conditions can introduce subtle bugs that are often difficult to reproduce. Insecurity-sensitive applications, this can provide attackers with opportunities to manipulate shared resources. For example, a banking application may allow unauthorized transactions if proper checks are not in place, potentially leading to significant financial loss.

Prevention Strategies

To avoid race conditions, developers can employ several strategies:

Synchronization Mechanisms: Utilize locks, mutexes, or semaphores to control access to shared resources. By ensuring that only one thread can access a resource at a time, developers can prevent inconsistent states.

Atomic Operations: Where possible, use atomic operations to perform read-modify-write sequences without interruption. These operations ensure that data is modified correctly even in a multithreaded environment.

Thread Safety: Design functions to be thread-safe by avoiding shared states or using concurrent data structures designed for multithreading environments.

Testing for Concurrency Issues: Implement stress testing and concurrency testing to expose potential race conditions. Tools that simulate high-load environments can be particularly useful in identifying issues that may not be present under typical conditions.

Developers can adopt best practices, leverage advanced programming techniques, and employ modern development tools to protect against these common vulnerabilities. By fostering a culture of security-minded programming, organizations can significantly reduce their risk exposure and build resilient software that stands the test of time. As the landscape of threats evolves, continual learning and adaptation will remain crucial elements in the development of secure software systems.

Chapter 5: Cryptography Basics in Rust

In this chapter, we will explore the basics of cryptography in the Rust programming language, leveraging its features to write safe and efficient cryptographic code.

5.1 Introduction to Cryptography

Cryptography is the science of encoding and decoding information to protect it from unauthorized access. The main objectives of cryptography are confidentiality, integrity, authentication, and non-repudiation.

There are two primary types of cryptographic techniques:

Symmetric Cryptography: A single key is used for both encryption and decryption. The major challenge is secure key distribution. Examples include AES (Advanced Encryption Standard) and DES (Data Encryption Standard).

Asymmetric Cryptography: This uses a pair of keys: a public key for encryption and a private key for decryption. Asymmetric schemes solve the key distribution problem. RSA (Rivest-Shamir-Adleman) and ECC (Elliptic Curve Cryptography) are popular examples.

5.2 Setting Up Rust for Cryptography

To implement cryptographic functions in Rust, we will use external libraries that provide tested and optimized cryptographic algorithms. The most commonly used library for cryptography in Rust is `rust- crypto`, along with others such as `ring` and `openssl`.

Install Rust: Ensure that you have Rust installed. If not, you can do so by running the following command:

```bash
curl --proto '=https' --tlsv1.2 -sSf https://sh.rustup.rs | sh
```

Create a new Cargo project: Use Cargo, Rust's package manager, to start a new project.

```bash
cargo new crypto_basics cd crypto_basics
```

Add Dependencies: Open `Cargo.toml` and add the cryptography library. For this chapter, let's use `aes`, `block-modes`, and `rand` for generating keys and randomness.

```toml
[dependencies] aes = "0.7"
block-modes = "0.8"
rand = "0.8"
```

5.3 Symmetric Cryptography with AES

AES is a widely used symmetric key encryption standard. We will create a simple example to demonstrate how to encrypt and decrypt data using AES in Rust.

```rust
use aes::Aes256;
use block_modes::{BlockMode, Cbc}; use block_modes::Plaintext;
```

```rust
use rand::Rng; use std::str;
type Aes256Cbc = Cbc<Aes256, Plaintext>; fn main() {
// Generate a random key
let key = rand::thread_rng().gen::<[u8; 32]>();
let iv = rand::thread_rng().gen::<[u8; 16]>();


let plaintext = b"The quick brown fox jumps over the lazy
dog";


// Encrypt the data
let cipher    =    Aes256Cbc::new_from_slices(&key,
&iv).unwrap();         let         cipher_text         =
cipher.encrypt_vec(plaintext);


// Decrypt the data
let cipher    =    Aes256Cbc::new_from_slices(&key,
&iv).unwrap();         let         decrypted_data         =
cipher.decrypt_vec(&cipher_text).unwrap();


println!("Original:                                    {}",
str::from_utf8(plaintext).unwrap()); println!("Ciphertext:
{:?}", cipher_text);

println!("Decrypted:                                    {}",
str::from_utf8(&decrypted_data).unwrap());
}
```
```
```

Explanation

Key and IV Generation: We create a random key and initialization vector (IV) required for AES encryption.

Encryption: Using the AES algorithm in CBC mode, we encrypt the plaintext.

Decryption: We initialize the cipher again with the same key and IV to decrypt the data. ### 5.4 Hashing

Hash functions take an input and produce a fixed-size string of bytes. They are commonly used in data integrity checks and password storage. Rust's `sha2` crate is a good library to perform hashing.

```toml
[dependencies] sha2 = "0.9"
```

Now, let's create a simple password hashing example:

```rust
use sha2::{Sha256, Digest};

fn hash_password(password: &str) -> Vec<u8> { let mut hasher = Sha256::new();


hasher.update(password); hasher.finalize().to_vec()
}
fn main() {

let password = "my_secure_password"; let hashed = hash_password(password);


println!("Password: {}", password);
```

70

```
println!("Hashed: {:x?}", hashed);
}
```
```

### 5.5 Key Takeaways

**Safety and Performance**: Rust's ownership model and type safety help ensure that cryptographic implementations are both safe and efficient.

**Standard Libraries**: Use established libraries instead of implementing cryptographic algorithms from scratch.

**Stay Updated**: Cryptography is a rapidly evolving field. Stay informed about the latest vulnerabilities and best practices such as using key stretching and proper salt generation for hashing.

By utilizing Rust's ecosystem of libraries, we can effectively implement secure cryptographic functions with confidence in their performance and safety. As the field of cryptography continues to evolve, it is crucial to stay updated and apply best practices in your implementations. In the next chapter, we will explore advanced cryptographic techniques and their applications.

# Introduction to Cryptographic Concepts and Their Applications

Cryptography is the science and art of securing communication and information from adversaries. It involves techniques for protecting the confidentiality, integrity, authenticity, and non-repudiation of data. At its
```

core, cryptography transforms readable data, known as plaintext, into an unreadable format called ciphertext using algorithms and keys. Only authorized parties, possessing the correct keys, can decrypt the ciphertext back into plaintext.

1.1.1 Types of Cryptography

Cryptography is generally classified into two broad categories:

Symmetric Cryptography: In symmetric cryptography, the same key is used for both encryption and decryption. This method is efficient in terms of speed but necessitates secure key distribution. Common examples include the Advanced Encryption Standard (AES) and the Data Encryption Standard (DES).

Asymmetric Cryptography: Also known as public-key cryptography, it utilizes a pair of keys: a public key for encryption and a private key for decryption. The public key can be shared openly, while the private key must be kept secret. RSA (Rivest-Shamir-Adleman) and Elliptic Curve Cryptography (ECC) are prominent examples.

1.1.2 Hash Functions

A crucial component of cryptographic systems is the hash function, which produces a fixed-size string of characters (the hash value) from an input of any size. Hash functions play a vital role in data integrity checks, digital signatures, and many other cryptographic applications. Examples of cryptographic hash functions include SHA-256 and MD5.

1.1.3 Digital Signatures

Digital signatures provide a method for validating the authenticity and integrity of a message. They utilize asymmetric cryptography, allowing a signer to produce a signature for a message using their private key. Recipients can verify the signature with the sender's public key, ensuring that the message originated from the stated sender and has not been altered in transit.

1.2 The Importance of Cryptography in Software Development

As digital communication proliferates, the demand for secure systems has risen dramatically. Effective cryptographic implementation is vital for protecting sensitive data, including personal information, financial records, and confidential communications. Inadequate security practices can lead to severe breaches, resulting in data loss, identity theft, and financial fraud.

Developers must have a solid understanding of cryptographic principles to design applications that are not only functional but also secure. This awareness is crucial in mitigating the risks associated with cyber threats, such as man-in-the-middle attacks, replay attacks, and data breaches.

1.3 Rust: A Modern Language for Secure Programming

Rust is a systems programming language that emphasizes safety, performance, and concurrency. Its robust memory management features, enforced at compile-time, help prevent many common vulnerabilities, such as buffer overflows and null pointer dereferences. As a result, Rust has emerged as an attractive choice for developers looking to implement cryptographic algorithms and protocols securely.

1.3.1 Features of Rust for Cryptography

Memory Safety: Rust's ownership model ensures memory safety without a garbage collector, making it an excellent choice for performance-critical applications, such as cryptographic systems, where every microsecond counts.

Concurrency: Rust's concurrency model helps avoid common concurrency pitfalls, allowing developers to safely write multi-threaded applications. This feature is paramount for applications that require efficient parallel processing of cryptographic operations.

Rich Ecosystem: The Rust ecosystem is continually growing, with numerous libraries dedicated to cryptography. Popular libraries like `rust-crypto`, `ring`, and `sodiumoxide` provide a wide range of algorithms and tools for secure communication.

Error Handling: Rust encourages explicit error handling, enabling developers to write code that gracefully manages exceptions encountered during encryption and decryption processes, which is particularly important in cryptographic contexts.

1.4 Applications of Cryptography in Rust Programming

Cryptography finds application across various domains, including:

Secure Communication: Rust can be used to build secure messaging apps utilizing TLS/SSL protocols to ensure private communication over the internet.

Data Encryption: Applications that handle sensitive user data can employ Rust's cryptographic libraries to encrypt data both at rest and in transit.

Blockchain and Cryptocurrencies: With the rise of

74

blockchain technology, Rust has gained traction for developing secure and efficient smart contracts and decentralized applications.

Digital Signatures: Rust is widely used to implement cryptographic systems that require the verification of identities and integrity of documents, such as legal contracts or software distribution.

Password Management: Creating secure password hashing functions in Rust can lead to better user authentication processes and protection against credentials stealing.

This chapter provides a foundation for exploring advanced cryptographic practices and their integration within Rust, setting the stage for developing secure applications in an increasingly interconnected world. Each subsequent chapter will build upon this foundational knowledge, guiding the reader through the intricacies of implementing cryptography in Rust software development.

Implementing Symmetric and Asymmetric Encryption in Rust

Encryption is a foundational technology for securing data, ensuring that only authorized parties can access or read sensitive information. In this chapter, we will explore how to implement symmetric and asymmetric encryption in the Rust programming language, focusing on strong cryptographic practices and leveraging the power of Rust's ecosystem.

Understanding Encryption Types

Before we dive into the implementation, it's crucial to understand the two types of encryption we will be discussing: symmetric and asymmetric encryption.

Symmetric Encryption

Symmetric encryption uses the same key for both encryption and decryption. This means that both the sender and recipient must securely share the key before communicating. Common symmetric encryption algorithms include AES (Advanced Encryption Standard) and ChaCha20.

Asymmetric Encryption

Asymmetric encryption, on the other hand, uses a pair of keys: a public key for encryption and a private key for decryption. This allows a sender to encrypt a message with the recipient's public key, ensuring that only the recipient, who possesses the corresponding private key, can decrypt and read the message. RSA and ECC (Elliptic Curve Cryptography) are two widely used asymmetric encryption algorithms.

Setting Up the Rust Environment for Cryptography

To implement encryption in Rust, we will utilize the `rust-crypto` and `rand` crates, which provide cryptographic functionality and random number generation, respectively. Make sure you have Rust installed on your machine. If you haven't set it up yet, you can do so from the [official Rust website](https://www.rust-lang.org/).

Create a new Rust project:

```bash
cargo new encryption_example cd encryption_example
```

```
```

Open `Cargo.toml` and add the necessary dependencies:

```toml
[dependencies]
aes = "0.7"
block-modes = "0.8"
rand = "0.8"
rsa = "0.5"
pkcs8 = "0.10"
```

Run `cargo build` to install the dependencies. ## Implementing Symmetric Encryption with AES

We will start our implementation with symmetric encryption using the AES algorithm. ### AES Encryption Example

Here, we will create a simple function to encrypt and decrypt messages using AES in CBC (Cipher Block Chaining) mode.

```rust
use aes::{Aes128, BlockEncrypt, BlockDecrypt, NewBlockCipher}; use block_modes::{BlockMode, Cbc};

use block_modes::block_padding::Pkcs7; use rand::Rng;

use std::iter::repeat_with;

type Aes128Cbc = Cbc<Aes128, Pkcs7>; fn generate_random_key() -> Vec<u8> {

let mut rng = rand::thread_rng();

repeat_with(|| rng.gen_range(0..=255)).take(16).collect()
```

```rust
}
fn encrypt_message(key: &[u8], plaintext: &[u8]) ->
Vec<u8> { let iv = generate_random_key();

let cipher = Aes128Cbc::new_from_slices(key,
&iv).unwrap(); let ciphertext =
cipher.encrypt_vec(plaintext);

[iv, ciphertext].concat()

}

fn decrypt_message(key: &[u8], ciphertext: &[u8]) ->
Vec<u8> { let (iv, ciphertext) = ciphertext.split_at(16);

let cipher = Aes128Cbc::new_from_slices(key,
iv).unwrap(); cipher.decrypt_vec(ciphertext).unwrap()

}

fn main() {

let key = generate_random_key();

let plaintext = b"Hello, Rust Encryption!";


let ciphertext = encrypt_message(&key, plaintext);
println!("Ciphertext: {:?}", ciphertext);

let decrypted_message = decrypt_message(&key,
&ciphertext);

println!("Decrypted Message: {:?}",
String::from_utf8(decrypted_message).unwrap());

}
```
```

### Explanation
```

Key Generation: We generate a random 16-byte key using the `rand` crate.

Encryption: In the `encrypt_message` function, we create an AES cipher instance and encrypt the plaintext, prepending the IV (Initialization Vector) to the ciphertext.

Decryption: The `decrypt_message` function extracts the IV from the ciphertext, initializes the cipher with it, and then decrypts the ciphertext.

Implementing Asymmetric Encryption with RSA

Next, we will implement asymmetric encryption using RSA. We will first generate a public/private key pair and then use them for encrypting and decrypting messages.

RSA Encryption Example

```rust
use rsa::{RsaPrivateKey, RsaPublicKey, PaddingScheme};
use rand::rngs::OsRng;

fn generate_rsa_keys() -> (RsaPrivateKey, RsaPublicKey) { let mut rng = OsRng;

let bits = 2048;


let private_key = RsaPrivateKey::new(&mut rng, bits).expect("failed to generate a key"); let public_key = RsaPublicKey::from(&private_key);


(private_key, public_key)
}
```

```rust
fn encrypt_with_rsa(public_key: &RsaPublicKey,
message: &[u8]) -> Vec<u8> { let padding =
PaddingScheme::new_pkcs1v15_encrypt();
public_key.encrypt(&mut OsRng, padding,
&message).expect("failed to encrypt")

}

fn decrypt_with_rsa(private_key: &RsaPrivateKey,
ciphertext: &[u8]) -> Vec<u8> { let padding =
PaddingScheme::new_pkcs1v15_encrypt();
private_key.decrypt(padding, &ciphertext).expect("failed
to decrypt")

}

fn main() {

let (private_key, public_key) = generate_rsa_keys(); let
message = b"Hello, Rust Asymmetric Encryption!";


let ciphertext = encrypt_with_rsa(&public_key, message);
println!("Ciphertext: {:?}", ciphertext);


let decrypted_message = decrypt_with_rsa(&private_key,
&ciphertext); println!("Decrypted Message: {:?}",
String::from_utf8(decrypted_message).unwrap());

}
```
```

### Explanation

**Key Generation**: We generate a 2048-bit RSA key
pair.
```

Encryption: The `encrypt_with_rsa` function encrypts a message using the public key and PKCS#1 v1.5 padding.

Decryption: Using the private key, the `decrypt_with_rsa` function retrieves the original message from the ciphertext.

Symmetric encryption with AES provides fast and efficient encryption for large volumes of data, while asymmetric encryption with RSA allows secure key exchange and ensures confidentiality between two parties without pre-sharing a key.

Chapter 6: Advanced Cryptographic Solutions with Rust

Cryptography serves as the backbone of internet security, enabling secure transactions, data privacy, and integrity. Rust, known for its performance and safety, has emerged as a compelling choice for implementing advanced cryptographic solutions. This chapter delves into the principles of cryptography and how Rust can be employed to implement these concepts effectively.

1. Cryptographic Fundamentals

Before we dive into Rust implementations, it's crucial to understand the basics of cryptography. At its core, cryptography transforms data into a format that is unreadable to unauthorized users. The main objectives of cryptography are:

Confidentiality: Ensuring that sensitive information remains secret.

Integrity: Verifying that data has not been altered.

Authentication: Providing proof of the origin of data.

Non-repudiation: Ensuring that a sender cannot deny sending a message. Cryptography techniques are generally categorized into two types:

1.1 Symmetric Cryptography

In symmetric cryptography, the same key is used for both encryption and decryption. The main challenge is how to securely share the key. Common symmetric algorithms include AES (Advanced Encryption Standard) and DES (Data Encryption Standard).

1.2 Asymmetric Cryptography

Asymmetric cryptography employs a pair of linked keys: a public key for encryption and a private key for decryption. This method allows secure key exchanges without sharing sensitive information directly.

Prominent asymmetric algorithms include RSA (Rivest-Shamir-Adleman) and ECC (Elliptic Curve Cryptography).

2. Rust and Cryptography

Rust has become a favored language for cryptographic applications due to its emphasis on safety and performance. The language's features, such as ownership, borrowing, and lifetimes, help eliminate common programming errors like buffer overflows and null pointer dereferences, which can lead to vulnerabilities in cryptographic systems.

2.1 Popular Rust Cryptography Libraries

Several libraries provide robust cryptographic functionalities in Rust. Notable among them are:

RustCrypto: This collection of cryptographic algorithms written in Rust provides a foundation for implementing various cryptographic schemes, ranging from hash functions to ciphers and public-key algorithms.

ring: A safe and fast crypto library designed for production use. It focuses on high-level cryptographic operations while still being efficient.

sodiumoxide: A Rust binding for the libsodium library, this library provides high-level cryptographic functions while maintaining security and usability.

3. Implementation of Cryptographic Solutions

Let's explore a couple of practical implementations to illustrate how to utilize Rust for advanced cryptographic solutions.

3.1 AES Encryption

Here is an example of how to implement AES encryption using the `aes` crate from RustCrypto.

```rust
// Cargo.toml
// [dependencies]
// aes = "0.7"
// block-modes = "0.8"
// hex = "0.4"
use aes::{Aes128, BlockEncrypt, NewBlockCipher}; use block_modes::{BlockMode, Cbc};

use block_modes::BlockMode as _; // Import BlockMode trait to enable .new_iv() method use hex;

use rand::Rng;

// AES encryption function

fn encrypt_aes(key: &[u8; 16], iv: &[u8; 16], data: &[u8]) -> Vec<u8> { let cipher = Cbc::<Aes128>::new_var(key,
```

```rust
iv).unwrap();
let ciphertext = cipher.encrypt_vec(data); ciphertext
}
// Example usage fn main() {
let key: [u8; 16] = rand::thread_rng().gen(); // Generate a random 128-bit key let iv: [u8; 16] = rand::thread_rng().gen(); // Generate a random IV
let data = b"Hello, world!";

let encrypted_data = encrypt_aes(&key, &iv, data); println!("Encrypted Data: {:?}", hex::encode(encrypted_data));
}
```

3.2 RSA Encryption and Signing

Implementing RSA encryption and signing involves using the `rsa` crate along with `rand` for generating keys:

```rust
// Cargo.toml
// [dependencies]
// rsa = "0.5"
// rand = "0.8"
use rsa::{RsaPrivateKey, RsaPublicKey, PaddingScheme};
use rand::rngs::OsRng;
fn main() {
```

```
let mut rng = OsRng;

// Generate a new RSA key pair let bits = 2048;

let private_key = RsaPrivateKey::new(&mut rng,
bits).expect("Failed to generate a key"); let public_key =
RsaPublicKey::from(&private_key);

// Message to encrypt

let msg = b"This is a secret message!";

// Encrypt the message

let padding = PaddingScheme::new_pkcs1v15_encrypt();

let enc_data = public_key.encrypt(&mut rng, padding,
&msg[..]).expect("Failed to encrypt");

// Decrypt the message

let padding = PaddingScheme::new_pkcs1v15_encrypt();

let dec_data = private_key.decrypt(padding,
&enc_data).expect("Failed to decrypt");

println!("Decrypted:                              {:?}",
String::from_utf8(dec_data).expect("Invalid UTF-8"));

}
```
```

## 4. Advanced Topics in Cryptography ### 4.1
Cryptographic Hash Functions

Hash functions play a critical role in data integrity. They
allow us to compute a fixed-size hash from input data,
which can be used to verify the integrity of that data. In
Rust, you can implement hash functions using the `sha2`
crate.
```

4.2 Digital Signatures

Digital signatures provide authentication and non-repudiation by allowing the sender to sign messages with their private key. Receivers can then verify the signature with the sender's public key.

4.3 Key Management

Secure key management is vital in any cryptographic system. Ensure keys are generated securely, stored in protected environments, and rotated regularly to mitigate the risks of exposure.

The examples provided showcase how to implement both symmetric and asymmetric cryptographic techniques effectively. As you continue your journey in cryptography with Rust, remember that security is a process—not just a product—requiring continuous assessment and improvement. With a solid understanding of cryptographic principles and Rust's capabilities, you are well-equipped to build secure systems that can withstand evolving threats in the digital landscape.

Building Custom Cryptographic Libraries in Rust

In addition to existing libraries, the need for custom cryptographic solutions tailored to specific applications is increasingly apparent. Rust, with its focus on safety, performance, and concurrency, is an excellent choice for building custom cryptographic libraries. This chapter will guide you through the principles and practices of developing your own cryptographic library in Rust.

1. Understanding the Basics of Cryptography

Before diving into Rust, it's essential to grasp core cryptographic concepts:

Symmetric Encryption: Uses the same key for both encryption and decryption. Examples include AES and ChaCha20.

Asymmetric Encryption: Uses a pair of keys—public and private. RSA and ECC (Elliptic Curve Cryptography) are common examples.

Hash Functions: Converts input data of any size into a fixed-size string, ensuring data integrity. SHA- 256 and BLAKE2 are widely used.

Digital Signatures: Provides a way to verify the authenticity and integrity of messages. Generally employs a combination of hashing and asymmetric encryption.

Understanding these fundamental concepts allows for making informed decisions about what features your library should implement.

2. Setting Up Your Rust Environment

To begin development, ensure you have Rust installed on your system. You can download Rust from [the official website](https://www.rust-lang.org/). Use `rustup` for managing Rust versions and toolchains, which simplifies package management and updates.

```bash
curl --proto '=https' --tlsv1.2 -sSf https://sh.rustup.rs | sh
```

Once installed, you can create a new project using Cargo, Rust's package manager and build system.

```bash
cargo new custom_crypto_lib cd custom_crypto_lib
```

3. Project Structure

A typical Rust project structure consists of the following components:

`src/`: Contains your source code, usually with a `lib.rs` file for library code and a `main.rs` for executable binaries.

`Cargo.toml`: The manifest file containing project metadata, dependencies, and versioning.

For our cryptographic library, we will work primarily within the `src/lib.rs` file. You can organize your code into modules to keep the functionality clean and maintainable.

4. Implementing a Basic Symmetric Encryption Algorithm ### 4.1. Choosing an Algorithm

For this example, we'll implement a simple symmetric encryption algorithm using the AES (Advanced Encryption Standard). However, instead of directly implementing AES, we can rely on existing libraries like

`aes` to handle the complexities.

Add the `aes` and `block-modes` as dependencies in your `Cargo.toml`:

```toml
[dependencies] aes = "0.7"
```

block-modes = "0.8"

block-padding = "0.2"

```
```

4.2. Basic AES Implementation

In `src/lib.rs`, set up the necessary imports and create a structure to manage encryption and decryption.

```rust
extern crate aes;

extern crate block_modes; extern crate block_padding;

use aes::{Aes128, BlockDecrypt, BlockEncrypt, NewBlockCipher}; use block_modes::{BlockMode, Cbc};

use block_padding::Pkcs7; use rand::Rng;

use std::fmt;

pub struct CustomCrypto { key: [u8; 16],

iv: [u8; 16],

}

impl CustomCrypto {

pub fn new(key: [u8; 16]) -> Self { let mut iv = [0u8; 16];
rand::thread_rng().fill(&mut iv[..]); Self { key, iv }

}

pub fn encrypt(&self, data: &[u8]) -> Vec<u8> { let cipher
= Aes128::new(&self.key.into());

let mut buffer = data.to_vec(); let pos = buffer.len();

buffer.resize(pos + 16, 0); // padding

Cbc::<Aes128, Pkcs7>::new(&cipher, &self.iv.into())

.encrypt(&mut buffer, pos)
```

```
.unwrap(); buffer
}

pub fn decrypt(&self, data: &[u8]) -> Vec<u8> { let cipher
= Aes128::new(&self.key.into());

let mut buffer = data.to_vec();

Cbc::<Aes128, Pkcs7>::new(&cipher, &self.iv.into())

.decrypt(&mut buffer)

.unwrap(); buffer

}

}
```
```

### 4.3. Explanation of Code

**Dependencies**: The example utilizes `aes`, `block-modes`, and `block-padding` for handling encryption and decryption effectively.

**Initialization Vector (IV)**: An IV is generated randomly each time an instance of `CustomCrypto` is created. Using a fresh IV for every encryption is vital for security.

**Encryption/Decryption**: The `encrypt` and `decrypt` functions manage the data transformation while ensuring proper padding.

## 5. Testing Your Library

It's essential to verify that your implementation functions as intended. You can write tests in Rust using the built-in test framework.
```

```rust
#[cfg(test)] mod tests {
use super::*;
#[test]
fn test_aes_encryption() { let key = [0u8; 16];
let crypto = CustomCrypto::new(key); let data = b"Hello,
Rust!";
let encrypted = crypto.encrypt(data);
let decrypted = crypto.decrypt(&encrypted);
assert_eq!(data, &decrypted[..data.len()]);
}
}
```

Run your tests using:
```bash
cargo test
```

6. Conclusion

Building a custom cryptographic library in Rust gives you not only the flexibility to tailor your solutions but also the performance and safety that Rust embodies. As cryptography plays a crucial role in securing data in modern applications, understanding how to implement these algorithms yourself can enhance both your knowledge and the security of your projects.

In this chapter, we've only scratched the surface by implementing a basic symmetric encryption algorithm. Further chapters could delve into more complex features such as digital signatures, key management, and performance optimization, providing a solid foundation for any cryptographic application.

Further Reading and Resources

"The Rust Programming Language" by Steve Klabnik and Carol Nichols

[Rust Crypto Libraries](https://github.com/RustCrypto)

Angle for cryptographic primitives and best practices in a real-world context and how to integrate them into larger applications.

By building and testing cryptographic libraries in Rust, you equip yourself with essential tools to tackle the important task of securing information. Moving forward, consider exploring and contributing to existing projects in the Rust ecosystem to further hone your skills and contribute to the community.

Rust-Based Implementations of Hashing Algorithms and Digital Signatures

Hashing algorithms and digital signatures serve as foundational components in securing information, ensuring data integrity, and validating authenticity across various domains. Rust, known for its performance and memory safety, offers an impressive environment for implementing these cryptographic constructs. This chapter delves into the Rust-based implementations of hashing algorithms and digital signatures, exploring their benefits, common libraries, and practical applications.

1. Understanding Hashing Algorithms

Hashing algorithms transform input data into a fixed-size string of characters, typically a digest that represents the unique essence of the input. The properties of a good hashing algorithm include:

Deterministic: The same input will always produce the same output.

Quick Computation: It should be computationally efficient to generate the hash.

Pre-image Resistance: Given a hash value, it should be infeasible to reconstruct the original input.

Collision Resistance: It should be difficult to find two different inputs that produce the same hash value.

Avalanche Effect: A small change in input should produce a drastically different hash.

1.1 Rust Libraries for Hashing

Rust has several libraries that facilitate secure and efficient hashing. Notable among them are:

`sha2`: This crate implements the SHA-2 family of hashing algorithms (including SHA-256 and SHA-512). It's widely used in various applications, including TLS and cryptocurrencies.

`blake2`: This crate provides an implementation of the BLAKE2 hash function, known for its speed and security. BLAKE2 is designed to be faster than MD5 while providing security comparable to SHA-3.

`ripemd`: Although less common, this library offers the RIPEMD family of hash functions, which can be useful for specific legacy applications.

With these libraries, developers can easily generate secure

hashes for passwords, file integrity checks, and more.

1.2 Example: Implementing SHA-256 in Rust

Here's a minimal example showcasing how to use the `sha2` crate for generating a SHA-256 hash.

```rust
use sha2::{Sha256, Digest};

fn main() {

let input = b"hello, world";

let mut hasher = Sha256::new();

hasher.update(input);

let result = hasher.finalize();


println!("SHA-256 hash: {:x}", result);

}
```

This implementation takes a simple string, computes its SHA-256 hash, and prints the result. The code is concise, efficient, and leverages Rust's memory safety features.

2. Digital Signatures

Digital signatures enable verification of authenticity and integrity of a message or document. They rely on asymmetric cryptography, where a private key is used to sign a message, and a corresponding public key is used for verification. The key properties of digital signatures include:

Authentication: Ensures that the sender is legitimate.

Integrity: Verifies that the message has not been altered.

Non-repudiation: The signer cannot deny having signed the message. ### 2.1 Rust Libraries for Digital Signatures

Rust provides several libraries for implementing digital signatures. Some of the prominent libraries include:

`ring`: A comprehensive library that supports various cryptographic operations including digital signatures using Ed25519 and RSA.

`ed25519-dalek`: Specifically designed for Ed25519 signatures, known for their efficiency and security.

`rust-crypto`: A versatile library offering a variety of cryptographic functions, including digital signature mechanisms.

2.2 Example: Implementing Digital Signatures in Rust

Here's a simple example using the `ed25519-dalek` library for creating and verifying digital signatures:

```rust
use ed25519_dalek::{Keypair, Signature, Signer, Verifier};
use rand::rngs::OsRng;

fn main() {
// Generate a random keypair let mut csprng = OsRng{};

let keypair = Keypair::generate(&mut csprng);

// Message to be signed

let message: &[u8] = b"This is a secret message.";
```

```
// Signing the message

let signature: Signature = keypair.sign(message);

// Verification

assert!(keypair.verify(message, &signature).is_ok());

// Print verification result println!("Signature verified successfully!");

}
```
```` ``` ````

In this example, we generate an Ed25519 key pair, sign a message, and then verify the signature. The use of Rust's type system ensures that operations are performed safely and efficiently.

3. Performance and Safety in Rust

One of the most appealing aspects of Rust for cryptographic implementations is its focus on performance and safety. The language's ownership model eliminates common bugs such as memory leaks and race conditions, making it ideal for cryptographic applications where precision and reliability are paramount.

3.1 Concurrency in Rust

Rust's emphasis on zero-cost abstractions and powerful concurrency features allows developers to write highly concurrent and safe cryptographic applications. Libraries like `async-std` and `tokio` enable developers to work with asynchronous operations, enhancing the performance of I/O-bound cryptographic tasks.

3.2 FFI and Interoperability
````

For systems that require interoperability with existing C libraries, Rust provides a Foreign Function Interface (FFI). This allows developers to leverage established cryptographic libraries while applying Rust's safety guarantees on their code.

4. Practical Applications

The implementations discussed in this chapter have practical applications that span various fields, including:

Blockchain and Cryptocurrency: Secure transactions rely heavily on hashing and digital signatures.

SSL/TLS: Secure communications over the internet use cryptographic algorithms to establish trust and integrity.

Data Integrity Checks: Hashing algorithms ensure that files and data packets have not been tampered with.

Identity Verification: Digital signatures are essential in authentication and identity verification processes.

Rust-based implementations of hashing algorithms and digital signatures represent a promising advancement in the field of cryptography. With its focus on safety, performance, and concurrency, Rust provides developers with the tools to create secure and fast cryptographic applications.

Chapter 7: Developing Secure Communication Tools in Rust

In this chapter, we'll explore how to leverage Rust's strengths to develop secure communication tools, covering foundational principles, practical implementations, and best practices.

7.1 The Importance of Secure Communication

Secure communication involves protecting the confidentiality, integrity, and authenticity of messages exchanged between parties. This is essential to prevent eavesdropping, data tampering, and impersonation. Common protocols and technologies used for secure communication include:

TLS (Transport Layer Security): Ensures encrypting data sent over networks.

PGP (Pretty Good Privacy): Provides encryption and signing for emails.

SSH (Secure Shell): Used for secure remote administration and file transfers.

Given the rise of malicious attacks and cyber threats, building secure communication tools is paramount. Rust's foundational principles of ownership, type safety, and concurrency make it an excellent choice for building systems that require such security guarantees.

7.2 Understanding Rust's Safety and Performance Features

Rust's memory safety guarantees, absence of a garbage collector, and zero-cost abstractions come together to create a language that is both safe and performant:

Ownership Model: Prevents data races at compile-time, which is crucial for concurrent secure communication applications.

Borrow Checker: Enforces strict rules on how data is accessed and shared, reducing errors that can lead to security vulnerabilities.

Type System: Enables better error handling and checks, making it easier to develop robust components to handle communication protocols.

These characteristics allow developers to focus on building secure features without the overhead of managing memory safety, which is often a pain point in languages such as C or C++.

7.3 Frameworks and Libraries for Secure Communication in Rust

Several Rust libraries can be leveraged to create secure communication tools. Below are some of the most relevant libraries:

7.3.1 `rustls`

`rustls` is a modern TLS library built to be safe, fast, and simple. It is written entirely in Rust and eliminates many of the potential security pitfalls found in other implementations. Using `rustls` makes it easy to set up secure TLS connections in your application.

Example:

```rust
use rustls::{ClientConfig, ClientSession, ServerName}; use
```

std::sync::Arc;

// Configure and build the TLS session here...
```
```

7.3.2 `tokio` and `tokio-tls`

`tokio` is an asynchronous runtime for Rust, designed for building fast network applications. Coupled with

`tokio-tls`, it allows for asynchronous and secure communication over TCP, which is ideal for applications requiring high throughput and low latency.

Example:

```rust

use tokio::net::TcpStream;

use tokio_native_tls::TlsStream;

// Establish a secure connection here...
```
```

### 7.3.3 `sodiumoxide`

`sodiumoxide` is a Rust binding of the popular libsodium library, which provides an easy-to-use interface for cryptographic operations. It includes functions for encryption, decryption, and signing, making it a great choice for implementing security features in communication tools.

```rust

use sodiumoxide::crypto::box_;  let (pk, sk) = box_::gen_keypair();
```
```

// Use the key pair for secure communication...
```
```

7.4 Designing a Secure Communication Tool

When developing secure communication tools, it's vital to follow a structured design approach: ### 7.4.1 Requirements Analysis

Identify the specific requirements of the communication tool. What data will be transmitted? Who are the users? What cryptographic protocols need to be followed?

7.4.2 Architecture

Design the tool's architecture with a focus on modularity and security. Consider separating application logic from encryption logic so that changes can be made easily without affecting the entire system.

7.4.3 Security Features Implementation Implement critical features such as:

End-to-End Encryption: Ensures that only intended users can read the messages.

Authentication: Verifies the identity of users to mitigate impersonation risks.

Data Integrity Checks: Protects against unauthorized modifications of messages. ### 7.4.4 Testing and Validation

Testing is crucial to the security of the tool. Conduct thorough unit tests, integration tests, and security audits. Engage in code reviews and consider employing fuzz testing to uncover potential vulnerabilities.

7.5 Best Practices for Secure Communication

Development

To ensure the security of the communication tool you are developing, follow these best practices:

Keep Security Libraries Updated: Security libraries frequently release updates to fix vulnerabilities; always use the latest version.

Adopt Crypto Best Practices: Use well-established cryptographic protocols and avoid custom implementations.

Implement Logging and Monitoring: Retain logs of communication events to help identify anomalous behavior.

Educate Users: Provide resources to help users understand the importance of secure communications and best practices.

Developing secure communication tools using Rust presents a compelling opportunity to combine performance with safety. By leveraging Rust's features alongside established libraries, you can create robust applications that protect user data against unauthorized access and attacks. As we move further into a future where digital privacy is paramount, mastering these tools in Rust will position developers at the forefront of secure software development.

Creating Secure Messaging Systems with End-to-End Encryption

This chapter explores how to create a secure messaging system using E2EE in Rust—the systems programming language known for its performance, safety, and concurrency. We'll delve into key concepts of encryption, implement foundational algorithms, and build a simplified messaging system that showcases how Rust can be used to create secure applications.

Understanding End-to-End Encryption ### What is End-to-End Encryption?

End-to-end encryption ensures that only the communicating users can read the messages exchanged between them. In an E2EE system, the messages are encrypted on the sender's device and can only be decrypted by the intended recipient's device. This means that even if a third party intercepts the messages, they cannot decipher the content without the correct decryption keys.

Importance of E2EE

Data Privacy: E2EE protects user data from unauthorized access.

Integrity: Ensures the message hasn't been altered in transit.

Authentication: Confirms the identities of the parties involved. ## Setting Up the Rust Environment

Before diving into the implementation, you need to set up your Rust environment.

Install Rust: If you haven't already, download and install Rust from [rust-lang.org](https://www.rust-lang.org/).

Create a New Project: Use Cargo to create a new project by running:

```bash

cargo new secure_messaging_system cd secure_messaging_system
```

Add Dependencies: We will use the `aes` crate for encryption and `rand` for generating secure random numbers. Add the following lines to your `Cargo.toml`:

```toml [dependencies] aes = "0.7"
block-modes = "0.8"

rand = "0.8"

hex = "0.4"
```

Implementing Encryption in Rust ### Key Generation

Key generation is the foundation of encryption. For our messaging system, we will generate symmetric keys for the AES encryption algorithm.

```rust
use rand::Rng;

fn generate_key() -> [u8; 16] {

let mut key = [0u8; 16]; // AES-128
```

```
rand::thread_rng().fill(&mut key); key
}
```
` ` `

Encrypting Messages

Using AES in Cipher Block Chaining (CBC) mode, we'll encrypt messages. Here is how we can implement the encryption function:

```rust
use aes::{Aes128, BlockEncrypt};

use aes::cipher::{NewCipher, BlockMode, Pkcs7};

use block_modes::{BlockMode as BlockModeTrait, Cbc};
type Aes128Cbc = Cbc<Aes128, Pkcs7>;

fn encrypt_message(key: &[u8], plaintext: &[u8]) -> Vec<u8> { let iv = rand::random::<[u8; 16]>(); // Random IV

let cipher = Aes128Cbc::new_from_slices(key, &iv).unwrap(); let mut buffer = plaintext.to_vec();

cipher.encrypt(&mut buffer, plaintext.len()).unwrap();


// Prepend IV for decryption let mut output = iv.to_vec(); output.append(&mut buffer); output
}
```
` ` `

Decrypting Messages

To ensure we can retrieve the original message, we need a decryption function as well:

````rust
fn decrypt_message(key: &[u8], ciphertext: &[u8]) ->
Vec<u8> { let (iv, data) = ciphertext.split_at(16);

let cipher = Aes128Cbc::new_from_slices(key,
iv).unwrap(); let mut buffer = data.to_vec();

cipher.decrypt(&mut buffer).unwrap(); buffer

}
````

Building the Messaging System

With our encryption and decryption functions ready, we
can now create a simple messaging system. The following
example demonstrates basic send and receive
functionalities.

````rust
struct Messenger { key: [u8; 16],

}

impl Messenger { fn new() -> Self {

Messenger {

key: generate_key(),

}

}

fn send_message(&self, message: &str) -> Vec<u8> {

let encrypted_message = encrypt_message(&self.key,
message.as_bytes()); encrypted_message

}
````

```rust
fn receive_message(&self, payload: &[u8]) -> String {

let decrypted_message = decrypt_message(&self.key,
payload);
String::from_utf8(decrypted_message).expect("Invalid
UTF-8")

}

}
```

Testing the Messaging System

To verify the functionality, we'll implement a simple main function:

```rust
fn main() {

let messenger = Messenger::new();


let message = "Hello, secure world!"; println!("Original
Message: {}", message);

let encrypted = messenger.send_message(message);
println!("Encrypted          Message:          {:?}",
hex::encode(&encrypted));


let decrypted = messenger.receive_message(&encrypted);
println!("Decrypted Message: {}", decrypted);

}
```

This chapter has walked you through the essentials of

building a secure messaging system using end-to-end encryption in Rust. You learned how to generate cryptographic keys, encrypt and decrypt messages using the AES algorithm, and encapsulated the functionalities into a simple messaging structure.

Implementing TLS/SSL Protocols in Rust

Transport Layer Security (TLS) and its predecessor, Secure Sockets Layer (SSL), are protocols that provide a secure communication channel over a computer network. These protocols are essential for protecting data integrity, confidentiality, and authentication in various applications, including web browsing, email, and virtual private networks. In this chapter, we'll explore how to implement TLS/SSL protocols in Rust, leveraging the language's strengths for safety, concurrency, and performance.

Why Rust?

Rust is a systems programming language that emphasizes memory safety, thread safety, and zero-cost abstractions. Given the critical nature of security protocols like TLS/SSL, the advantages of using Rust become apparent. The language's expressive type system helps eliminate common programming errors such as buffer overflows or null pointer dereferencing—vulnerabilities that can be exploited in network communications. Thus, Rust provides an ideal environment for implementing a robust and secure TLS/SSL solution.

Setting Up the Environment

Before diving into the implementation, we need to set up our Rust environment and include the required dependencies. Ensure that you have Rust installed. You can check this by running:

```bash
rustc --version
```

Once Rust is installed, create a new Cargo project:

```bash
cargo new tls_ssl_example cd tls_ssl_example
```

Adding Dependencies

To work with TLS/SSL in Rust, we will utilize the `rustls` and `tokio` libraries, which provide an efficient way to implement secure network protocols. Update your `Cargo.toml` to include these dependencies:

```toml
[dependencies]
tokio = { version = "1", features = ["full"] } rustls = "0.21"
tokio-rustls = "0.23"
```

Understanding the Basics of TLS/SSL

Before we commence with the implementation, it is vital to understand the basic elements of the TLS/SSL protocol:

Handshake: This is the initial phase where the client and server establish parameters for communication, share security credentials, and agree on encryption methods.

Data Transfer: Once the handshake is complete, data can be securely exchanged using the negotiated parameters.

Closure: This phase involves closing the connection securely. ## Implementing a Simple TLS Client and Server

Creating a TLS Server

Let's create a basic TLS server that listens for incoming connections. Create a new file named `server.rs` with the following code:

```rust
use std::{sync::Arc, fs::File, io::{BufReader, Write}, net::SocketAddr}; use tokio::{net::TcpListener, io::{AsyncWriteExt, AsyncReadExt}};

use tokio_rustls::{TlsAcceptor, rustls::{Certificate, PrivateKey, ServerConfig}}; use rustls_pemfile::{read_all, PEM};

#[tokio::main]
async fn main() -> Result<(), Box<dyn std::error::Error>> { let addr = "127.0.0.1:8443".parse::<SocketAddr>()?;

let certs = load_certs("certs/server.crt")?;

let key = load_private_key("certs/server.key")?;


let mut config = ServerConfig::new(rustls::NoClientAuth::new()); config.set_single_cert(certs, key)?;

let acceptor = TlsAcceptor::from(Arc::new(config));
```

```rust
let listener = TcpListener::bind(&addr).await?;
println!("TLS server running on {:?}", addr);
loop {
    let (stream, _) = listener.accept().await?; let acceptor = acceptor.clone();


    tokio::spawn(async move {
        let mut tls_stream = acceptor.accept(stream).await.unwrap(); let mut buf = vec![0; 1024];
        let n = tls_stream.read(&mut buf).await.unwrap();
        tls_stream.write_all(&buf[..n]).await.unwrap();
    });
}
}
fn load_certs(filepath: &str) -> Result<Vec<Certificate>, std::io::Error> { let certs = &mut Vec::new();
    let file = File::open(filepath)?;
    for cert in read_all(&mut BufReader::new(file))? {
        certs.push(Certificate(cert));
    }
    Ok(certs)
}


fn load_private_key(filepath: &str) -> Result<PrivateKey, std::io::Error> { let mut keys = vec![];
```

```rust
    let file = File::open(filepath)?;
    for key in read_all(&mut BufReader::new(file))? {
        if let PEM::RSA_PRIVATE_KEY(key) | PEM::EC_PRIVATE_KEY(key) = key {
            keys.push(PrivateKey(key));
        }
    }
    Ok(keys.remove(0))
}
```

Creating a TLS Client

Next, let's create a simple TLS client that connects to our server. Create a file named `client.rs` with the following content:

```rust
use tokio::net::TcpStream;

use tokio_rustls::TlsConnector;

use rustls::{ClientConfig, ServerName}; use std::sync::Arc;

use std::fs::File;

use std::io::{BufReader};

use rustls_pemfile::{read_one, PEM};

#[tokio::main]

async fn main() -> Result<(), Box<dyn std::error::Error>> { let config = ClientConfig::new();
```

113

```rust
let connector = TlsConnector::from(Arc::new(config)); let
addr = "127.0.0.1:8443".parse::<SocketAddr>()?;


let stream = TcpStream::connect(addr).await?;

let                    domain                    =
ServerName::try_from("localhost").unwrap();

let  mut  tls_stream  =  connector.connect(domain,
stream).await?;              tls_stream.write_all(b"Hello,
server!").await?;

let mut buffer = vec![0; 1024];

let  n  =  tls_stream.read(&mut   buffer).await?;
println!("Received:                              {}",
String::from_utf8_lossy(&buffer[..n]));


Ok(())

}
```

Generating Certificates

To run the server and client, SSL certificates are required.
You can generate self-signed certificates using OpenSSL.
Run the following commands in your terminal:

```bash
# Generate a private key

openssl genrsa -out certs/server.key 2048
```

```
# Generate a self-signed certificate
openssl req -new -x509 -key certs/server.key -out
certs/server.crt -days 365 -subj "/CN=localhost"
```

Ensure that the certificates are stored in a `certs` directory within your project root. ## Running the Example

With the server and client implemented, you can now run them in separate terminal windows:

In one terminal, run the server:

```bash
cargo run --bin server
```

In another terminal, run the client:

```bash
cargo run --bin client
```

You should see the server receiving a message from the client and sending a response back.

In this chapter, we implemented a simple TLS server and client using Rust. We highlighted the strengths of Rust in ensuring safety and performance while managing complex protocols like TLS/SSL. As you develop deeper applications requiring encryption and security, Rust's ecosystem provides a robust foundation for secure networked communication. As you move forward, consider exploring more advanced features such as client authentication, session resumption, and integrating additional security measures to fortify your applications.

Chapter 8: Vulnerability Detection and Mitigation in Rust

This chapter delves into vulnerability detection and mitigation within Rust programming, exploring the language's features, tooling, and best practices to secure applications.

8.1 Understanding Vulnerabilities

Before diving into Rust's methodologies for vulnerability detection and mitigation, it is essential to comprehend common types of vulnerabilities that can plague software systems:

Memory Safety Issues: These include buffer overflows, use-after-free, and double free vulnerabilities, frequently associated with languages that allow manual memory management.

Data Races: Concurrency issues that arise when multiple threads access shared data without proper synchronization, leading to unpredictable results.

Input Validation Flaws: Vulnerabilities that occur when software fails to validate user input correctly, enabling injection attacks and cross-site scripting.

Rust tackles these concerns head-on through its innovative design and built-in safety features. ## 8.2 Rust's Safety Features

8.2.1 Ownership and Borrowing

At the core of Rust's memory safety is the ownership system. Each value in Rust has a single owner, and memory is freed when that owner is out of scope. This eliminates common issues like dangling pointers and use-after-free errors. Borrowing allows functions to temporarily access a value without taking ownership, and Rust enforces strict rules around mutable and immutable borrowing to prevent data races.

8.2.2 Lifetimes

Lifetimes in Rust ensure that references are valid as long as they are used. By annotating lifetimes, developers can help the compiler determine the relationships between different scopes, preemptively catching potential memory safety issues at compile time.

8.2.3 Concurrency

Rust's concurrency model allows safe parallel processing through its ownership and type system. The `Send` and `Sync` traits ensure that data is accessed in a thread-safe manner, preventing data races at compile time.

8.3 Tools for Vulnerability Detection

While Rust's design minimizes many vulnerabilities, proactive detection and mitigation strategies remain crucial. Several powerful tools exist to aid developers in identifying potential vulnerabilities:

8.3.1 Clippy

Clippy is a collection of lints to catch common mistakes and improve performance. By integrating Clippy into the development workflow, developers can receive immediate feedback on potential issues that may arise within their code.

8.3.2 Rust Analyzer

An interactive development environment (IDE) tool that enhances Rust code insight. Rust Analyzer provides real-time suggestions and can identify potential code vulnerabilities, ensuring a smoother and safer coding experience.

8.3.3 Miri

Miri is an experimental interpreter for Rust that can detect various categories of undefined behavior, including data races. By using Miri during the testing phase, developers can identify and address problems that may not surface in regular testing.

8.3.4 Sanitizers

Rust can leverage existing sanitizers, like AddressSanitizer and ThreadSanitizer, to catch memory errors and data races at runtime. Incorporating these tools can enhance the robustness of the application during testing phases.

8.4 Best Practices for Vulnerability Mitigation

While Rust's features significantly reduce the likelihood of vulnerabilities, developers should adopt several best practices to further bolster security:

8.4.1 Regular Code Reviews

Engaging peers in code reviews can surface overlooked issues and foster a culture of shared responsibility for code quality and security.

8.4.2 Adopting Dependency Management Strategies

Rust's package manager, Cargo, allows developers to manage dependencies effectively. It's critical to regularly update dependencies and audit them for known vulnerabilities, utilizing tools like `cargo audit` to maintain a secure application.

8.4.3 Utilizing Explicit Error Handling

Rust employs a robust error handling model, making it essential to embrace Result and Option types judiciously. Explicitly handling errors instead of panicking can prevent application crashes and allow for graceful degradation in functionality.

8.4.4 Continuous Integration and Testing

Setting up continuous integration (CI) pipelines that include automated testing can help catch vulnerabilities early in the development cycle. Incorporating fuzz testing can further uncover hidden edge cases and potential security flaws.

Vulnerability detection and mitigation in Rust programming require a multifaceted approach, combining the language's inherent safety features with best development practices and robust tooling. By understanding the common vulnerabilities, leveraging Rust's safety mechanisms, and employing a proactive security mindset, developers can significantly enhance the security posture of their applications.

Building Tools to Detect Common Vulnerabilities in Applications

However, ensuring the security of Rust applications demands more than just leveraging the language's features; it requires robust tools for detecting vulnerabilities during development. This chapter explores the strategies and techniques for building tools aimed at identifying common vulnerabilities in Rust applications, equipping developers with the capability to create safer software.

1. Understanding Common Vulnerabilities in Software

Before diving into tool development, we must first understand the common vulnerabilities prevalent in software applications. The Open Web Application Security Project (OWASP) provides a well-regarded list of common vulnerabilities that include:

Injection Attacks: Occurs when an application embeds untrusted data into a command or query.

Broken Authentication: Exploitation due to weak authentication mechanisms.

Sensitive Data Exposure: Insufficient protection of sensitive data.

Cross-Site Scripting (XSS): Injection of malicious scripts into a web application.

Security Misconfiguration: Incorrect security settings leading to exploitable vulnerabilities.

In Rust, while many of the lower-level vulnerabilities (such as buffer overflow) are mitigated by the language itself, high-level issues such as logic flaws, race conditions, and improper error handling can still arise. Thus, effective detection mechanisms are crucial.

2. The Benefits of Rust for Secure Programming

Rust's design promotes secure programming in several ways:

Ownership Model: Rust's ownership model enforces strict borrowing rules, reducing the risk of race conditions and ensuring memory safety.

Type System: Its powerful type system catches many errors at compile time, such as mismatched types and invalid operations.

Concurrency Support: Built-in concurrency primitives minimize issues related to thread safety, providing solid foundations for writing concurrent applications.

Despite these advantages, the need for vulnerability detection tools remains paramount. Developers must be equipped to handle logical errors and other vulnerabilities that are not inherently prevented by Rust.

3. Building Static Analysis Tools

Static analysis tools analyze source code without executing it, identifying potential vulnerabilities through pattern matching, control flow analysis, and data flow analysis. To build a basic static analysis tool for Rust, consider the following steps:

3.1. Setting Up the Environment

To create a static analysis tool, set up a Rust development environment. This involves installing the Rust toolchain and choosing a framework for parsing Rust code. Rust's `syn` crate is a popular choice for syntax parsing.

3.2. Parsing Rust Code

Utilize `syn` to parse Rust files and construct an Abstract Syntax Tree (AST). Here's a simple example of parsing a Rust source file:

```rust
```

```rust
use std::fs; use syn::File;

fn parse_file(file_path: &str) -> File {

let source = fs::read_to_string(file_path).expect("Unable
to read file"); syn::parse_file(&source).expect("Unable to
parse file")

}
```

3.3. Identifying Vulnerabilities

Once you have the AST, you can traverse it to find
potential vulnerabilities. For instance, to detect instances
of unsafe code blocks which could lead to undefined
behavior:

```rust
fn    check_for_unsafe(node:    &syn::Item)    {    if    let
syn::Item::Fn(func) = node {

if func.attrs.iter().any(|attr| attr.path.is_ident("unsafe"))
{ println!("Unsafe function detected: {}", func.sig.ident);

}

}

}
```

3.4. Reporting and Metrics

Provide detailed feedback regarding any detected
vulnerabilities, including their location and description.
This makes it easier for developers to understand and
rectify issues promptly.

4. Developing Dynamic Analysis Tools

Dynamic analysis involves examining a running application to detect vulnerabilities during execution. Tools like Valgrind and Instrumentation frameworks can be paralleled in a Rust environment. Here's a basic approach:

4.1. Instrumentation

Instrument the Rust application to log data on memory usage, data races, and assertion failures. Rust's feature `#[cfg(test)]` can help you run tests that validate application behavior under expected conditions.

4.2. Fuzz Testing

Fuzz testing generates random input data to expose vulnerabilities. The `cargo-fuzz` crate can be integrated into Rust projects to facilitate fuzz testing. Here's a simple way to get started with fuzzing:

Set up `cargo-fuzz` by installing it:

```bash
cargo install cargo-fuzz
```

Add a fuzz target:

```rust
#[fuzz_target(start = "fuzz_input")] fn fuzz_input(input:
&[u8]) {
// Your function to test with input
```

```
}
```
```

### 4.3. Monitoring and Logging

Implement logging mechanisms to trace program execution and monitor for abnormal behavior during dynamic analysis. Leverage existing logging frameworks, like `log` or `env_logger`.

## 5. Integrating Security Throughout the Development Lifecycle

To maximize the effectiveness of vulnerability detection tools, integrate them into the development lifecycle:

**Code Reviews**: Automate vulnerability detection during code reviews.

**Continuous Integration**: Include static and dynamic analysis tools in CI/CD pipelines to enforce practices that minimize vulnerabilities.

**Educate Developers**: Provide resources and training on secure coding practices and how to utilize the tools effectively.

By harnessing Rust's inherent features and creating targeted static and dynamic analysis tools, developers can significantly reduce risks associated with software vulnerabilities. This chapter has outlined key strategies for creating these tools, emphasizing the need for continuous integration and education in secure coding practices.
```

Writing Rust Code to Prevent SQL Injection, XSS, and Other Attacks

In this chapter, we will explore how to write Rust code that effectively prevents SQL Injection, XSS, and other common web application vulnerabilities.

Understanding the Threats ### SQL Injection

SQL Injection occurs when an attacker is able to manipulate a query by injecting malicious SQL code into an input field. This can lead to unauthorized access to data, data corruption, or even complete compromise of the database.

Cross-Site Scripting (XSS)

XSS is a security vulnerability that allows attackers to inject malicious scripts into web pages viewed by other users. This can result in the theft of session cookies, redirection to malicious sites, or various other harmful actions performed in a user's session.

Other Attacks

In addition to SQL Injection and XSS, developers must be cognizant of other attacks, such as Cross-Site Request Forgery (CSRF), command injection, and insecure direct object references. This chapter will focus primarily on SQLi and XSS, but the principles discussed will also assist in preventing these other forms of attack.

Rust's Strengths

Rust is designed with memory safety and concurrency as key features. The strong type system and ownership model of Rust help prevent many common programming errors that can lead to vulnerabilities. Furthermore, the language encourages developers to think critically about how data is handled, making it easier to write secure code.

Preventing SQL Injection in Rust

To effectively prevent SQL Injection in Rust, it is crucial to use parameterized queries. The `diesel` crate, a popular ORM for Rust, provides a simple interface that allows you to execute SQL commands safely.

Example: Using Diesel to Prevent SQL Injection

```rust
use diesel::prelude::*;

use diesel::sql_types::Text;

#[derive(Queryable)] struct User {

id: i32, name: String,

}


fn find_user_by_name(conn: &SqliteConnection, user_name: &str) -> QueryResult<User> { use crate::schema::users::dsl::*;

// Parameterized query using diesel users

.filter(name.eq(user_name))

.first::<User>(conn)

}
```

In this example, we're using the `filter` method from

Diesel's DSL (domain-specific language) to create a parameterized query. The `eq` method ensures that user input is treated as a value rather than part of the SQL command, effectively mitigating the risk of SQL Injection.

Best Practices for SQL Injection Prevention

Use ORM Libraries: Rely on libraries like Diesel or SQLx, which inherently utilize parameterized queries.

Avoid Dynamic Queries: Minimize the use of concatenated SQL queries. Stick to prepared statements through your ORM.

Validate Input: Ensure input data types align with expected formats. ## Preventing Cross-Site Scripting (XSS) in Rust

Preventing XSS requires careful handling of user-generated content. In Rust, you can achieve this by ensuring proper encoding of output displayed in HTML.

Example: Encoding Output in Rust

When using web frameworks such as `warp` or `actix-web`, you should ensure that any output that comes from user input is properly escaped.

```rust
use warp::Filter;

#[tokio::main] async fn main() {

let route = warp::path("greet")

.and(warp::get())

.and(warp::query::<HashMap<String, String>>())

.map(|params: HashMap<String, String>| {
```

```
let              name                =
params.get("name").unwrap_or(&"Stranger".to_string());
let safe_name = warp::html::escape(name); // Escaping
the output format!("Hello, {}!", safe_name)

});

warp::serve(route).run(([127, 0, 0, 1], 3030)).await;

}
```
` ` `

In this example, we're escaping the output using
`warp::html::escape`, ensuring that any HTML tags
within the user input are rendered harmless rather than
executed.

Best Practices for XSS Prevention

Use Encoding Libraries: Always encode user input
before rendering it.

Content Security Policy (CSP): Implement CSP
headers to mitigate the impact of XSS if it occurs.

Sanitize Input: Use well-known libraries to sanitize
user input to remove potentially dangerous scripts.

Additional Security Practices ### Input Validation

Always validate all input data on both the client and the
server side to ensure that they conform to expected
formats. Use regular expressions and validation libraries
as necessary.

Secure Session Management

Implement secure session management practices. Use
secure cookies, set HttpOnly and Secure flags, and ensure

proper expiration and invalidation of sessions.

Regular Updates

Keep dependencies updated to their latest versions. Security vulnerabilities are often fixed in newer releases, and it's crucial to ensure that your application is not using outdated libraries with known issues.

Writing secure Rust code is an essential skill for modern application development. Understanding and implementing the strategies outlined in this chapter will significantly reduce the risk of SQL Injection, XSS, and other common web threats. Remember, security is an ongoing process; continually review and update your code, learn from incidents, and keep abreast of best practices and emerging threats. By fostering a security-first mindset, you will not only protect your applications but also instill confidence among your users.

Chapter 9: Creating Secure APIs with Rust

This chapter delves into how to harness the power of Rust, a systems programming language known for its focus on safety and performance, to create secure APIs. We will explore the various aspects of API development with Rust, including best practices, libraries, and tools to enhance security.

9.1 Understanding the Importance of API Security

APIs serve as the bridges that connect different applications, facilitating communication and data sharing. They are often targets for malicious attacks due to the sensitive data they handle. Common security threats to APIs include:

Injection Attacks: Malicious data input can manipulate the API's behavior.

Authentication Vulnerabilities: Weak authentication mechanisms can allow unauthorized access.

Data Exposure: Insufficient encryption can lead to sensitive data being exposed.

Rate Limiting Issues: Lack of proper controls can result in denial-of-service attacks.

Understanding the common threats is the first step in building a secure API. To effectively defend against these threats, a strong foundation in security best practices is essential.

9.2 Setting Up a Rust Development Environment

Before we can dive into API development, we need to set

131

up a Rust environment. Rust's built-in package manager, Cargo, simplifies the process of managing dependencies.

9.2.1 Installing Rust

To install Rust, follow these steps:

Open a terminal.

Run the following command to download the Rust installer:

```bash
curl --proto '=https' --tlsv1.2 -sSf https://sh.rustup.rs | sh
```

Follow the instructions provided in the installer to complete the installation.

Ensure Cargo and Rust are added to your system path by running:

```bash
source $HOME/.cargo/env
```

Verify the installation by checking the version:

```bash
rustc --version
```

9.2.2 Creating a New Project

You can create a new Rust project using Cargo:

```bash
cargo new secure_api cd secure_api
```

This command creates a new directory named `secure_api` containing a basic Rust application structure. ## 9.3 Building a Simple RESTful API

In this section, we will build a simple RESTful API using the popular Rust web framework, Actix-web. This framework is known for its speed and flexibility, making it a suitable choice for creating secure APIs.

9.3.1 Adding Dependencies

Edit your `Cargo.toml` file to include the following dependencies:

```toml
[dependencies] actix-web = "4.0"

serde = { version = "1.0", features = ["derive"] } serde_json = "1.0"

dotenv = "0.15"
```

9.3.2 Creating the API

In `src/main.rs`, we will set up a basic Actix-web server with route handling:

```rust

use actix_web::{web, App, HttpServer, HttpResponse, Responder, middleware}; use serde::{Serialize, Deserialize};

#[derive(Serialize, Deserialize)] struct User {
```

```rust
id: u32, name: String,
}
// In-memory user storage (for simplicity) static mut
USERS: Vec<User> = Vec::new();
async fn get_users() -> impl Responder { unsafe {
HttpResponse::Ok().json(&USERS)
}
}
async fn add_user(new_user: web::Json<User>) -> impl
Responder { unsafe {
USERS.push(new_user.into_inner());
}
HttpResponse::Created()
}
#[actix_web::main]
async fn main() -> std::io::Result<()> {
dotenv::dotenv().ok(); // Load environment variables
HttpServer::new(|| { App::new()
.wrap(middleware::Logger::default()) // Enable logging
.route("/users", web::get().to(get_users))
.route("/users", web::post().to(add_user))
})
.bind("127.0.0.1:8080")?
.run()
```

```
.await
}
```
` ` `

This code sets up a basic server with two endpoints: `GET /users` to retrieve users and `POST /users` to add new users.

9.4 Securing the API

9.4.1 Input Validation and Sanitization

One fundamental aspect of API security is validating and sanitizing all incoming data. In our previous example, we used Serde for deserializing JSON data, but we need to enhance security by adding validation checks to ensure the data received is safe and as expected.

```rust
fn validate_user(user: &User) -> Result<(), &'static str> {
if user.name.is_empty() {
Err("Name cannot be empty")
} else {
Ok(())
}
}
```
` ` `

Call `validate_user` in the `add_user` function before adding new entries. ### 9.4.2 Authentication and Authorization

Implementing proper authentication and authorization

mechanisms is crucial. We can use JSON Web Tokens (JWT) for secure authentication, allowing users to prove their identity when accessing the API.

Here's a basic example of how JWT could be checked: First, add the `jsonwebtoken` dependency in `Cargo.toml`:

```toml
jsonwebtoken = "8.1"
```

Then implement token verification logic:

```rust
use jsonwebtoken::{decode, encode, DecodingKey, EncodingKey, Header, Validation};

fn verify_token(token: &str) -> bool {

let decoding_key = DecodingKey::from_secret("your_secret_key".as_ref());
let validation = Validation::default();

decode::<User>(&token, &decoding_key, &validation).is_ok()

}

async fn protected_route(token: String) -> impl Responder { if verify_token(&token) {

HttpResponse::Ok().body("Access granted.")

} else {

HttpResponse::Unauthorized().body("Access denied.")
```

```
}

}
```
```

### 9.4.3 Rate Limiting

To prevent abuse and mitigate denial-of-service attacks, implement rate limiting using a third-party middleware like `actix-limiter`. This allows you to set limits on the number of requests that can be made to your API in a given timeframe.

### 9.4.4 Logging and Monitoring

Implement logging using `actix-web`'s built-in logging middleware. Ensure that you log failed authentication attempts, access patterns, and anomalies to facilitate monitoring and auditing.

## 9.5 Testing the API

Security testing is an essential step in the development lifecycle. Use tools like Postman or automated testing libraries to simulate requests and validate the API's behavior under various conditions.

### 9.5.1 Writing Unit Tests in Rust

Utilize Rust's built-in testing framework by adding tests for the API routes in a separate module:

```rust
#[cfg(test)] mod tests {

use super::*;

use actix_web::{test, App};

#[actix_web::test]
```
```

```
async fn test_get_users() {
```

```
let app = test::init_service(App::new().route("/users",
web::get().to(get_users))).await;      let      req      =
test::TestRequest::get().uri("/users").to_request();
```

```
let            resp:            Vec<User>            =
test::call_and_read_body_json(&app,        req).await;
assert_eq!(resp.len(), 0);
```

```
}
```

```
}
```

```
` ` `
```

We covered setting up a simple RESTful API with Actix-web, implementing input validation, security mechanisms such as JWT, rate limiting, and effective logging practices. Security is an ongoing process; continuous monitoring and updating will help ensure the resilience of your API against evolving threats.

Designing and Implementing Secure RESTful APIs

RESTful APIs, in particular, have gained immense popularity due to their simplicity and scalability. However, with great power comes great responsibility, and ensuring the security of these APIs has become an essential focus for developers.

In this chapter, we delve into the principles of designing and implementing secure RESTful APIs, covering best practices, potential vulnerabilities, and strategies for mitigating risks. Whether you are building an API for internal use or as a service exposed to external clients, this guide aims to equip you with the knowledge needed to safeguard your API against common threats.

Understanding Threats to RESTful APIs

Before delving into design and implementation, it is crucial to understand the various threats that RESTful APIs face. Common vulnerabilities include:

Unauthorized Access: Attackers may attempt to access restricted resources without proper permissions, leading to data breaches.

Data Exposure: Insufficient data protection measures can lead to the exposure of sensitive information.

Injection Attacks: SQL injection or other forms of code injection can compromise the integrity of your API.

Rate Limiting Abuse: Attackers may attempt to overwhelm your API with excessive requests, leading to denial-of-service conditions.

Man-in-the-Middle Attacks: Data transmitted over unencrypted channels is susceptible to interception.

Insecure Data Storage: Storing sensitive information insecurely can lead to data leaks.

Improper Input Validation: Failure to properly validate input can pave the way for various attacks.

Understanding these vulnerabilities is the first step in building a robust security posture for your API. ## Best Practices for Designing Secure RESTful APIs

1. Secure Communication

Use HTTPS: Always use HTTPS to encrypt data in

transit. This protects against man-in-the-middle attacks and ensures the integrity and confidentiality of the data being exchanged.

2. Authentication and Authorization

Token-based Authentication: Implement token-based authentication (such as OAuth 2.0 or JWT) to protect API endpoints. This ensures that only authenticated users can access specific resources.

Role-Based Access Control (RBAC): Define user roles and permissions to implement fine-grained access control. This limits access to resources based on user roles, enhancing security.

3. Input Validation and Data Sanitization

Strict Input Validation: Validate and sanitize all inputs to prevent injection attacks. Define strict data types and limits for inputs.

Use Whitelists: Instead of blacklisting, use whitelisting for allowed input formats to eliminate unforeseen vulnerabilities.

4. Rate Limiting and Throttling

Implement Rate Limiting: Set limits on the number of requests a user can make to your API in a defined timeframe. Use tokens or IP addresses to maintain usage quotas.

Throttling: Slow down the client's response if they exceed the allowed request limit. This can help mitigate denial-of-service attacks.

5. Logging and Monitoring

Comprehensive Logging: Implement logging for all API requests and responses. Capture data such as timestamps, endpoints accessed, IP addresses, and response codes.

Monitoring: Use monitoring tools to analyze logs for unusual patterns that may indicate malicious activity. Set up alerts for specific actions or thresholds.

6. Error Handling

Generic Error Messages: Avoid disclosing sensitive information through error messages. Provide generic responses that do not reveal whether an API endpoint exists or what may have gone wrong.

Log Errors: Use logging to track errors internally, while providing minimal information to end-users. ### 7. Versioning

Version Your API: Implement versioning to manage changes while maintaining the security of older versions. This allows clients to transition smoothly while ensuring security patches are applied to newer versions.

Implementing Security in Your API

After establishing a solid design foundation, the following steps outline the implementation process of security measures in your RESTful API:

Step 1: Choose the Right Frameworks and Libraries

Select frameworks that provide built-in security features. For example, many web frameworks come with built-in mechanisms for authentication, input validation, and logging.

Step 2: Implement Authentication and Authorization

Set up your chosen authentication method (e.g., OAuth 2.0 with token issuance).

Integrate authorization checks on each endpoint to ensure users have sufficient permissions before performing actions.

Step 3: Configure HTTPS

Use certificates issued by a trusted Certificate Authority (CA) to establish HTTPS.

Redirect all HTTP traffic to HTTPS to enforce secure communication. ### Step 4: Apply Rate Limiting and Throttling

Use middleware or API gateway features to enforce rate limiting and throttling. Set appropriate thresholds based on usage patterns.

Step 5: Utilize Input Validation Libraries

Leverage existing libraries to perform rigorous input validation. Regularly update these libraries to mitigate known vulnerabilities.

Step 6: Test and Audit Security

Conduct regular security testing, including penetration tests and vulnerability scans, to identify any weaknesses in your API. Periodically review your security policies and practices to keep them up to date.

Building secure RESTful APIs is essential in today's connected world. By understanding security principles, implementing best practices, and staying vigilant against emerging threats, developers can create robust APIs that protect sensitive data while providing reliable services.

Authenticating and Authorizing API Requests in Rust

This chapter delves into the processes of authentication and authorization while building APIs in Rust, a systems programming language renowned for its performance and safety, particularly in concurrent applications.

1. Introduction to Authentication and Authorization

Before delving into the practical aspects, it is essential to understand the distinction between authentication and authorization:

Authentication is the process of verifying the identity of a user or system. It ensures that users or systems are who they claim to be.

Authorization is the process of determining whether an authenticated user or system has permission to access specific resources or perform certain actions.

In the context of API development, both processes are vital for securing the application and ensuring that only the right users can access or modify resources.

2. Choosing an Authentication Method

When building APIs, selecting an appropriate authentication method is the first crucial step. Common methods include:

API Keys: Simple identifiers that a client uses to access an API. They are often passed as query parameters or HTTP headers.

OAuth 2.0: A widely adopted framework that allows third-party applications to delegate access to resources. It supports different grant types, including authorization code and client credentials.

JSON Web Tokens (JWT): A compact way to securely transmit information between parties as a JSON object. JWTs are commonly used for stateless authentication.

Example: Using JWT for Authentication

In this section, we will illustrate how to implement JWT-based authentication using Rust with a simple API example.

2.1 Setting Up the Environment Make sure to initialize a new Rust project:

```bash
cargo new rust_api_auth cd rust_api_auth
```

Add necessary dependencies in `Cargo.toml`:

```toml
[dependencies] actix-web = "4"

jsonwebtoken = "7"

serde = { version = "1", features = ["derive"] } serde_json = "1"
```

2.2 Defining the User Structure

Let's create a user struct and define our JWT claims:

```rust
use serde::{Deserialize, Serialize};
```

144

```rust
#[derive(Serialize, Deserialize)] struct Claims {
sub: String, exp: usize,
}
```

2.3 Creating a Token

We will create an endpoint for users to log in and get a token:

```rust
use actix_web::{web, HttpResponse, HttpServer, App};
use jsonwebtoken::{encode, Header};

use std::time::{SystemTime, Duration};

async fn login() -> HttpResponse {

let user_id = "user123"; // Example user ID let expiration = SystemTime::now()

.duration_since(SystemTime::UNIX_EPOCH)

.unwrap()

+ Duration::new(3600, 0); // Token valid for 1 hour

let claims = Claims {

sub: user_id.to_string(),

exp: expiration.as_secs() as usize,

};

let token = encode(&Header::default(), &claims, "your_secret_key".as_ref()).unwrap();
HttpResponse::Ok().json(token)

}
```

```
```

2.4 Running the Server

Now we'll set up the HTTP server to expose our login endpoint:

```rust #[actix_web::main]
async fn main() -> std::io::Result<()> {
HttpServer::new(|| {
App::new()
.route("/login", web::get().to(login))
})
.bind("127.0.0.1:8080")?
.run()
.await
}
```

Compile and run the server:

```bash cargo run
```

You can test the login endpoint using [curl](https://curl.se/) or Postman, expecting a JWT token in response. ## 3. Adding Authorization

Now that we have a basic authentication system in place, the next step is to implement authorization to protect our API routes.

3.1 Middleware for Token Validation

We need a middleware function to validate the JWT token and extract user information from it:

```rust
use actix_web::{middleware, web, HttpRequest, HttpResponse};

async fn validate_jwt(req: HttpRequest) -> Result<HttpRequest, HttpResponse> { let token = req.headers().get("Authorization")
.and_then(|h| h.to_str().ok())
.and_then(|h| h.strip_prefix("Bearer "))
.ok_or_else(|| HttpResponse::Unauthorized())?; let validation = jsonwebtoken::Validation::default();
// Verify the token (assuming `your_secret_key` is the same used during token creation)
let token_data = jsonwebtoken::decode::<Claims>(token, "your_secret_key".as_ref(), &validation)
.map_err(|_| HttpResponse::Unauthorized())?;
req.extensions_mut().insert(token_data.claims); Ok(req)
}
```

3.2 Protecting API Endpoints

Now, we can use our middleware to protect specific routes that require authorization:

```rust
async fn protected_route(req: HttpRequest) ->
```
147

```rust
HttpResponse {

// Access user information from the Claims

let claims = req.extensions().get::<Claims>().unwrap();
HttpResponse::Ok().json(format!("Hello,    user    {}!",
claims.sub))

}

#[actix_web::main]

async    fn    main()    ->    std::io::Result<()>    {
HttpServer::new(|| {

App::new()

.wrap_fn(validate_jwt)

.route("/protected", web::get().to(protected_route))

})

.bind("127.0.0.1:8080")?

.run()

.await

}
```
```

Authenticating and authorizing API requests effectively is essential for securing your applications. In this chapter, we explored how to implement JWT-based authentication and enhance it with authorization mechanisms in Rust using the Actix framework.

The approach demonstrated shows how robust security can be achieved with minimal setup. As always, ensure that you protect sensitive information, keep your
```

dependencies updated, and follow best practices when handling security keys and certificates.

Chapter 10: Implementing Secure Data Storage in Rust

Whether you're working on a personal project or developing an enterprise application, adopting best practices for secure data storage is crucial. Rust, a systems programming language known for its performance and safety features, offers many tools and techniques for implementing secure data storage solutions. This chapter will explore the fundamental principles of secure data storage and demonstrate how to leverage Rust's capabilities to build robust, secure applications.

10.1 Fundamentals of Secure Data Storage

Before diving into the practical implementation aspects, it is essential to understand the core principles that underlie secure data storage:

Confidentiality: Ensures that sensitive information is accessible only to those authorized to view it. This often involves encryption both at rest (data stored on disk) and in transit (data being transmitted).

Integrity: Assures that data has not been altered or tampered with. Mechanisms like checksums or hashes can be implemented to maintain data integrity.

Availability: Guarantees that data is accessible when needed. This requires reliable storage solutions, regular backups, and strategies for data recovery.

Authentication and Authorization: Ensures that users can be authenticated, and proper access controls are in place to limit data access based on user roles.

By understanding these principles, we can outline a

strategy for implementing secure data storage in Rust. ## 10.2 Security Features of Rust

Rust provides several features that make it an ideal choice for secure data storage:

Ownership and Borrowing: Rust's ownership model prevents data races and ensures memory safety, making it easier to manage sensitive data without the risk of unintended mutations or access.

Zero-cost Abstractions: Rust enables developers to implement complex security features without incurring runtime penalties, allowing for efficient data storage mechanisms.

Libraries and Ecosystem: The Rust ecosystem boasts several libraries designed for encryption, serialization, and secure file handling, making it easier to implement secure solutions.

10.3 Setting Up a Secure Data Storage Environment

To implement secure data storage in Rust, we will need to set up a working environment. Ensure you have the following:

Rust Installed: Ensure you have the latest version of Rust installed on your system. You can download it from the official [Rust website](https://www.rust-lang.org/).

Add Dependencies: We will use several crates such as `serde`, `serde_json`, and `aes` for data serialization and encryption. Open your `Cargo.toml` file and include the following dependencies:

```toml [dependencies]

serde = { version = "1.0", features = ["derive"] }
```

```
serde_json = "1.0"
aes = "0.7"
block-modes = "0.8"
rand = "0.8"
```

10.4 Implementing Encryption

One of the primary methods to ensure confidentiality is encryption. In this section, we'll implement simple AES encryption to secure data before storing it.

10.4.1 Key Generation

Generate a secure encryption key using a random number generator.

```rust
use rand::Rng;

use aes::{Aes128, BlockEncrypt, NewBlockCipher}; use block_modes::{BlockMode, Cbc};

use block_modes::block_padding::Pkcs7;

const AES_KEY_LEN: usize = 16; // 128 bits fn generate_key() -> [u8; AES_KEY_LEN] {

let mut key = [0u8; AES_KEY_LEN]; rand::thread_rng().fill(&mut key[..]); key

}
```

10.4.2 Data Encryption and Decryption

Next, let's implement functions to encrypt and decrypt

data using AES in CBC mode.

```rust
fn encrypt_data(key: &[u8], data: &[u8]) -> Vec<u8> { let
iv = rand::thread_rng().gen::<[u8; 16]>();

let cipher = Cbc::<Aes128, Pkcs7>::new_var(key,
&iv).unwrap(); let ciphertext = cipher.encrypt_vec(data);

[iv.to_vec(), ciphertext].concat()

}
fn decrypt_data(key: &[u8], data: &[u8]) -> Vec<u8> { let
(iv, ciphertext) = data.split_at(16);

let cipher = Cbc::<Aes128, Pkcs7>::new_var(key,
iv).unwrap(); cipher.decrypt_vec(ciphertext).unwrap()

}
```

10.4.3 Example Usage

Now, let's put everything together, demonstrating how to
encrypt and decrypt data securely.

```rust
fn main() {

let key = generate_key();

let data = b"Sensitive information";

let encrypted_data = encrypt_data(&key, data);

let decrypted_data = decrypt_data(&key,
&encrypted_data);
```

```rust
    assert_eq!(data.to_vec(), decrypted_data); println!("Data
    encrypted and decrypted successfully!");
}
```

10.5 Storing and Retrieving Data Securely

Once we have our encryption mechanisms, we need to focus on how to store this data securely. This involves choosing a secure file format and ensuring that sensitive metadata is not exposed.

10.5.1 Using JSON for Storage

Storing data in JSON format simplifies serialization but requires careful handling of sensitive information.

```rust
fn store_data(file_path: &str, key: &[u8], data: &[u8]) {
let encrypted = encrypt_data(key, data);

let              json_data              =
serde_json::to_string(&encrypted).unwrap();
std::fs::write(file_path, json_data).unwrap();

}

fn load_data(file_path: &str, key: &[u8]) -> Vec<u8> {

let              json_data              =
std::fs::read_to_string(file_path).unwrap();

let         encrypted:         Vec<u8>         =
serde_json::from_str(&json_data).unwrap();
decrypt_data(key, &encrypted)

}
```

```
```

10.5.2 Example File I/O

We can demonstrate the storage and retrieval process with a full example.

```rust
fn main() {

let key = generate_key();

let data = b"Sensitive information"; let file_path = "secure_data.json";

store_data(file_path, &key, data);

let retrieved_data = load_data(file_path, &key);

assert_eq!(data.to_vec(), retrieved_data); println!("Data stored and retrieved successfully!");

}

```
```

10.6 Best Practices for Secure Data Storage

Regularly Update Dependencies: Ensure libraries and crates are regularly updated to mitigate vulnerabilities.

Store Keys Securely: Never hard-code encryption keys. Use environment variables or secure vaults.

Implement Access Controls: Enforce strict file permissions to limit access to encrypted data.

Backup Encrypted Data: Regular backups are crucial, but always encrypt backup data as well.

155
```

Monitor and Audit: Implement logging and monitoring to detect unauthorized access or anomalies.

By leveraging Rust's unique features and following best practices, developers can create applications that protect sensitive information from unauthorized access and ensure data integrity. Through practical implementations of encryption, serialization, and secure file handling, you've gained the tools necessary to start building secure applications in Rust. As security threats evolve, continuous learning and adapting to new best practices will be essential in maintaining secure data storage solutions.

Encrypting Databases and File Systems with Rust

This chapter delves into the methodologies, libraries, and practical implementations of encrypting databases and file systems using Rust programming language. Leveraging Rust's performance, safety features, and strong typing can lead to robust cryptographic solutions that can seamlessly integrate with data storage systems.

5.1 Understanding Encryption

Before diving into implementation, it's critical to comprehend the fundamentals of encryption. At its core, encryption involves converting data into an unreadable format, which can only be transformed back into its original form through decryption. Two primary types of encryption exist:

Symmetric Encryption: This involves using the same key for both encryption and decryption. It is fast and suitable for encrypting large amounts of data but requires secure key management.

Asymmetric Encryption: This uses a pair of keys—a public key for encryption and a private key for decryption—allowing for secure data exchange without needing to share a secret key.

Rust has a variety of crates (libraries) that provide the functionality needed for both symmetric and asymmetric encryption, such as `aes`, `rustls`, and `ring`.

5.2 Setting Up Your Rust Environment

Before we can execute any encryption techniques, ensure that you have Rust installed on your machine. You can install it from the official website at [rust-lang.org](https://www.rust-lang.org/). Once installed, create a new project using Cargo, Rust's package manager and build system:

```bash
cargo new encrypt_db_fs cd encrypt_db_fs
```

Add necessary crates to your `Cargo.toml` file:

```toml
[dependencies] aes = "0.7"

block-modes = "0.8"

rand = "0.8"

serde = { version = "1.0", features = ["derive"] } sled = "0.34" # for lightweight database
```

5.3 Symmetric Encryption in Rust

In this section, we will implement symmetric encryption using the AES (Advanced Encryption Standard) algorithm. We'll focus on encrypting and decrypting files stored on the file system and simulating database- like storage using the Sled crate.

5.3.1 Encrypting and Decrypting Files

First, let's define functions for encrypting and decrypting files. We will use AES in CBC (Cipher Block Chaining) mode, which requires an initialization vector (IV) and a key.

```rust
use aes::{Aes128, BlockEncrypt, BlockDecrypt}; use block_modes::{BlockMode, Cbc};

use block_modes::BlockModeInstance; use rand::Rng;

use serde::{Serialize, Deserialize}; use std::fs::File;

use std::io::{Read, Write}; use std::path::Path;

use rand::rngs::OsRng;

type Aes128Cbc = Cbc<Aes128, block_modes::block_padding::Pkcs7>; fn generate_key() -> [u8; 16] {

let mut key = [0u8; 16]; OsRng.fill(&mut key); key

}

fn encrypt_file(path: &Path, key: &[u8; 16]) -> std::io::Result<()> { let iv = rand::random::<[u8; 16]>();
```

```rust
let mut file = File::open(path)?; let mut contents =
Vec::new(); file.read_to_end(&mut contents)?;

let cipher = Aes128Cbc::new_var(key, &iv).unwrap(); let
encrypted_data = cipher.encrypt_vec(&contents);

let mut output_file = File::create(format!("{}.enc",
path.display()))?;                output_file.write_all(&iv)?;
output_file.write_all(&encrypted_data)?;

Ok(())
}
fn decrypt_file(path: &Path, key: &[u8; 16]) ->
std::io::Result<()> { let mut file = File::open(path)?;

let mut iv = [0u8; 16]; file.read_exact(&mut iv)?;

let mut contents = Vec::new(); file.read_to_end(&mut
contents)?;

let cipher = Aes128Cbc::new_var(key, &iv).unwrap();

let                   decrypted_data                   =
cipher.decrypt_vec(&contents).unwrap();

let mut output_file = File::create(format!("{}.dec",
path.display()))?;
output_file.write_all(&decrypted_data)?;
```

```rust
    Ok(())
}
```

5.3.2 Integrating with a Simple Database

Next, let's create a simple interface that allows us to store and retrieve encrypted data using Sled, a modern embedded database designed for performance.

```rust
#[derive(Serialize, Deserialize)] struct UserData {

name: String, email: String,

}

fn save_user(db: &sled::Db, key: &[u8; 16], user_data: UserData) -> Result<(), sled::Error> { let serialized_data = bincode::serialize(&user_data).unwrap();

let mut encrypted_data = encrypt_vec(&serialized_data, key);


db.insert(user_data.email.as_bytes(), encrypted_data)?;
Ok(())

}

fn load_user(db: &sled::Db, key: &[u8; 16], email: &str) -> Result<UserData, sled::Error> { if let Some(encrypted_data) = db.get(email.as_bytes())? {

let                   decrypted_data                =
```

```rust
    decrypt_vec(&encrypted_data.to_vec(), key)?;

    let user_data: UserData = bincode::deserialize(&decrypted_data).unwrap();
    Ok(user_data)
    } else {

    Err(sled::Error::InvalidKey)

    }

    }
```

In this example, we create methods to encrypt and save user data to the database and retrieve and decrypt it when needed.

5.4 Asymmetric Encryption

Asymmetric encryption can be employed for secure key exchange and ensuring data integrity. In Rust, the

`ring` crate allows the usage of RSA and other asymmetric algorithms. Here's a brief example of generating key pairs:

```rust
use ring::{rand, signature};

fn generate_key_pair() -> (signature::RsaKeyPair, signature::RsaPublicKey) { let rng = rand::SystemRandom::new();

let pkcs8_bytes = signature::RsaKeyPair::generate_pkcs8(&rng, 2048).unwrap(); let keypair = signature::RsaKeyPair::from_pkcs8(pkcs8_bytes.as_ref() ).unwrap(); let public_key = keypair.public_key();
```

```
(keypair, public_key)
}
```
```

## 5.5 Best Practices for Secure Implementation

**Key Management:** Use secure methods to store and manage cryptographic keys. Consider employing hardware security modules (HSMs) or environment variables.

**Data Sanitization:** Ensure your program verifies the integrity and validity of the data before processing.

**Documentation & Compliance:** Follow industry standards and regulations (like GDPR, HIPAA) and document the encryption mechanisms used in your application.

**Regular Updates:** Keep your libraries and dependencies updated to avoid known vulnerabilities.

**Testing:** Regularly test your encryption practices and perform security audits to discover any potential weaknesses.

By embracing these methodologies, developers can ensure that their applications maintain high data security standards, safeguarding sensitive information from unauthorized access. As Rust continues to gain traction within the software development community, its capabilities in cryptography offer a promising path for secure and high-performance systems.
```

Building Secure Backup and Recovery Tools

Data loss, whether due to hardware failures, ransomware attacks, or accidental deletions, can have devastating effects. Thus, the design and implementation of backup tools that prioritize security while maintaining performance and usability is of utmost importance. This chapter focuses on building such tools using Rust, a modern programming language known for its performance and memory safety.

1. Why Rust?

1.1 Performance and Efficiency

Rust's performance characteristics make it an ideal choice for systems-level programming. Its zero-cost abstractions and fine-grained control over memory allocation ensure that backup processes, which often require handling large volumes of data, can operate with minimal overhead.

1.2 Safety and Concurrency

Rust's ownership model eliminates many common programming errors, such as buffer overflows and data races. This safety is critical in applications that deal with sensitive data. Additionally, Rust's support for concurrent programming allows us to design tools that can run backup operations alongside other system processes efficiently.

1.3 Ecosystem and Libraries

The Rust ecosystem includes a wealth of libraries for handling tasks like file I/O, cryptography, and network communication. Libraries like `serde` for serialization, `tokio` for asynchronous programming, and `ring` for cryptography provide the building blocks needed to implement secure and efficient backup solutions.

2. Designing Secure Backup and Recovery Tools ### 2.1 Defining Requirements

Before diving into implementation, we need to define the core requirements of our backup and recovery tool:

Data Integrity: Verify that data remains unchanged during backup and recovery processes.

Security: Encrypt data both in transit and at rest.

Usability: Provide an easy-to-use command-line interface (CLI) or GUI.

Recovery Speed: Ensure quick restoration of data when needed.

Scalability: Support backups for various sizes, from a single file to an entire system. ### 2.2 Architecture Overview

A well-structured architecture typically includes the following components:

Backup Engine: Manages the backup processes, including scheduling and execution.

Storage Interface: Handles interactions with various storage backends (local, cloud, or network).

Encryption Module: Ensures that data is encrypted during transit and at rest.

Logging and Monitoring: Provides logs for actions taken and monitors the success/failure of backups. ## 3. Implementation

164

3.1 Setting Up the Rust Project

Start by creating a new Rust project:

```bash
cargo new secure_backup_tool cd secure_backup_tool
```

3.2 Dependencies

Add the necessary dependencies in `Cargo.toml`:

```toml
[dependencies]
tokio = { version = "1.0", features = ["full"] } serde = { version = "1.0", features = ["derive"] } serde_json = "1.0"

ring = "0.16"
```

3.3 Building the Core Components #### 3.3.1 Backup Engine

The backup engine is responsible for managing backup tasks. Below is a simplified version of what this might look like:

```rust
use tokio::fs;

use std::path::Path;

async fn backup_file(source: &Path, destination: &Path) -> std::io::Result<()> { fs::copy(source, destination).await?;

Ok(())

}
```

```rust
// Example usage in main function #[tokio::main]
async fn main() {
let source = Path::new("data.txt");

let destination = Path::new("backup/data.txt");

if let Err(e) = backup_file(&source, &destination).await {
eprintln!("Failed to back up file: {}", e);
}
}
```

3.3.2 Encryption Module

Integrate encryption with the `ring` crate to ensure data is encrypted before storage:

```rust
use ring::aead::{self, Aad, BoundKey, Nonce, UnboundKey, OPEN, seal_in_place, split_at_mut}; use ring::rand::SystemRandom;


fn encrypt_data(plaintext: &[u8], key: &[u8], nonce: &[u8]) -> Vec<u8> {

let unbound_key = UnboundKey::new(&aead::CHACHA20_POLY1305, key).unwrap(); let nonce = Nonce::assume_unique_for_key(nonce);

let mut in_out = plaintext.to_vec();

let ad = Aad::from(&b"additional data"[..]);

let mut sealing_key: BoundKey =
```

unbound_key.new_bound_key();   seal_in_place(&mut
sealing_key, nonce, ad, &mut in_out, aead::Aad::len());

in_out

}
``` `

3.4 User Interface

Creating a simple CLI for the backup tool can be achieved
using the `clap` crate. Here's an example:

```toml [dependencies]
clap = { version = "3.0", features = ["derive"] }
```

```rust
use clap::{Arg, Command};

fn main() {
let matches = Command::new("Secure Backup Tool")
.version("0.1.0")
.about("Backup your files securely")
.arg(Arg::new("source")
.about("The source file to back up")
.required(true)
.index(1))
.arg(Arg::new("destination")
.about("The destination for the backup")
.required(true)
```
```

```
        .index(2))
        .get_matches();
    let source = matches.value_of("source").unwrap();
    let                 destination                 =
matches.value_of("destination").unwrap();
    // Initiate backup operation...
    }
```

4. Testing and Validation

Security and reliability are paramount in backup tools. Rigorous testing, including unit tests, integration tests, and security audits (e.g., testing for vulnerabilities like SQL injection or buffer overflows) are essential. Utilize Rust's built-in testing framework:

```rust
#[cfg(test)] mod tests {
    use super::*;
    #[test]
    fn test_encryption() { let key = [0u8; 32]; let nonce = [0u8; 12];
    let plaintext = b"The quick brown fox jumps over the lazy dog"; let encrypted_data = encrypt_data(plaintext, &key, &nonce);
    assert!(!encrypted_data.is_empty());
    // Additional tests for decryption can also be implemented
    }
```

```
}
```
```
```

By carefully designing the architecture, implementing reliable components, and conducting thorough testing, developers can create robust solutions that provide peace of mind against data loss. As threats to data integrity continue to evolve, tools must adapt to include stronger security practices, making Rust an excellent choice for future-proofing backup solutions.

Conclusion

In this journey through the compelling intersection of Rust programming and cybersecurity, we've explored the powerful capabilities of Rust as a language designed for performance and safety. From the foundational principles of writing secure code to the intricate implementation of advanced cryptographic solutions, it is clear that Rust is not just a tool, but a paradigm shift for developers dedicated to creating secure systems.

We began our exploration by understanding the core tenets of Rust's ownership model, which inherently reduces memory-related vulnerabilities such as buffer overflows and data races. By leveraging Rust's strengths, developers can write code that minimizes security risks while maintaining high performance—an essential aspect of modern cybersecurity.

As we delved into the specifics of secure coding practices, we emphasized the importance of adopting security as a fundamental principle throughout the software development life cycle (SDLC). Utilizing Rust's features, such as strong type systems and exhaustive pattern matching, can help in crafting code that is both efficient and resilient against attacks. This transformative approach ensures that security considerations are not an afterthought but an intrinsic part of the development process.

The latter sections of the book provided a comprehensive look at advanced cryptography within Rust. Understanding concepts such as symmetric and asymmetric encryption, hashing algorithms, and digital signatures is crucial for any cybersecurity professional. By employing libraries and tools native to the Rust ecosystem, such as `rustcrypto` and `ring`, we have highlighted practical ways to implement robust cryptographic solutions that can withstand the evolving threats of the digital landscape.

As this book draws to a close, we encourage you to view Rust not only as a programming language but as a vital asset in your cybersecurity toolkit. The knowledge and skills acquired throughout these chapters equip you to confront the growing challenges in cybersecurity with confidence, awareness, and strategic foresight.

In a world where vulnerabilities and attacks continue to proliferate, your role as a developer and a cybersecurity practitioner is more crucial than ever. By embracing the principles outlined in this book, you can contribute to building systems that are not only functional but also fundamentally secure.

We look forward to seeing how you apply these insights in your own projects and endeavors. The journey toward secure coding and advanced cryptographic solutions is ongoing; stay curious, keep learning, and commit to excellence in the ever-evolving field of cybersecurity.

Thank you for joining us on this exploration of Rust programming for cybersecurity. Together, let's pave the way for a safer, more secure digital future.

Biography

Jeff Stuart is a visionary writer and seasoned web developer with a passion for crafting dynamic and user-centric web applications. With years of hands-on experience in the tech industry, Jeff has mastered the art of problem-solving through code, specializing in Rust programming and cutting-edge web technologies. His expertise lies in creating efficient, scalable, and secure solutions that push the boundaries of what web applications can achieve.

As a lifelong learner and tech enthusiast, Jeff thrives on exploring the ever-evolving landscape of programming languages and frameworks. When he's not immersed in writing code or brainstorming innovative ideas, you'll find him sharing his knowledge through inspiring content that empowers others to unlock their full potential in the digital world.

Beyond his professional pursuits, Jeff enjoys exploring the art of minimalist design, reading thought-provoking books on technology and philosophy, and hiking to recharge his creative energies. His unwavering dedication to excellence and his belief in the transformative power of technology shine through in every page of his work, making this book a compelling guide for anyone eager to master the art of Rust programming and web development.

Glossary: Rust Programming for Cybersecurity

A

Allocation: The process of reserving a portion of memory for use by a program. Rust uses a system of ownership with rules that the compiler checks at compile time, preventing common memory issues through controlled allocation.

Asynchronous: A model of concurrent programming that allows for non-blocking operations. Rust provides async functions that let programs handle multiple tasks at once, which can be particularly useful for applications requiring high performance and responsiveness in cybersecurity tasks.

B

Borrow Checker: A component of Rust's compiler that enforces the rules of ownership and borrowing at compile time. It ensures that references to data do not outlive the data they refer to, thus preventing data races and dangling pointers.

Buffer Overflow: A common vulnerability that occurs when data overflows from one buffer to another, potentially allowing attackers to overwrite memory and execute arbitrary code. Rust mitigates this risk by providing strong type safety and bounds checking.

C

Cargo: The Rust package manager and build system. It simplifies the process of managing dependencies, building packages, and distributing Rust applications. In cybersecurity, Cargo makes it easier for developers to incorporate security libraries and tools into their projects.

Crate: A package of Rust code. It can be a library or a binary. Crates are the primary way to share reusable code in Rust, and many security-related libraries are available in the ecosystem, enhancing the language's utility in secure programming.

D

Data Race: A concurrency problem that occurs when two or more threads access shared data at the same time, and at least one of them modifies the data. Rust's ownership model prevents data races at compile time, making concurrent programming safer.

E

Endpoint Security: A cybersecurity approach that focuses on protecting endpoints or end-user devices from threats. Rust can be used to develop lightweight, efficient agents to monitor and protect endpoints due to its performance characteristics.

Error Handling: Rust emphasizes safe error handling using the `Result` and `Option` types, which help developers manage potential failures without panicking. This principle helps build resilient applications in cybersecurity that can gracefully recover from errors.

F

Function Pointer: A variable that stores the address of a function that can be invoked later in the code. Rust's strict typing makes it safer to use function pointers compared to some other languages, reducing the risk of vulnerabilities.

G

Garbage Collection: A form of automatic memory management that reclaims memory occupied by objects that are no longer in use. Rust does not use a garbage collector; it opts for ownership and borrowing, which maximizes performance and reduces runtime overhead, thus being preferred in security-critical applications.

H

Heap: A region of a process's memory used for dynamic memory allocation. In Rust, the `Box<T>` type allows developers to allocate data on the heap while retaining ownership, providing a controlled way to manage memory in cybersecurity applications.

I

Immutable: A property of data that prevents it from being modified after it is created. Rust embraces immutability by default, which can help mitigate the risk of unintended data alterations and enhance application stability.

Intrusion Detection System (IDS): A security solution that monitors for unauthorized access or attacks. Rust can be utilized to create high-performance IDS solutions due to its efficiency and concurrency support.

M

Mutex: A synchronization primitive that can be used to manage access to shared data across threads. Rust's `Mutex` type ensures that only one thread can access shared data at a time, preventing race conditions.

O

Ownership: A set of rules that governs how memory is managed in Rust, ensuring that there are no data races or memory leaks. The ownership model is crucial for developing secure applications that handle sensitive data.

P

Panic: A condition that occurs when a program encounters an unrecoverable error. Rust's approach to handling panics helps developers create robust applications that can safely handle failure scenarios without crashing.

Pointer: A variable that holds the memory address of another variable. Rust uses several kinds of pointers (e.g., references, smart pointers) to provide safety and prevent common issues like null pointer dereferencing.

R

Runtime: The period during which a program is executing. Rust aims for 'zero-cost abstractions', meaning that abstractions in the language do not incur additional runtime costs, making it suitable for performance-critical security applications.

S

Static Analysis: The process of analyzing source code without executing it to identify potential vulnerabilities or code quality issues. Rust's type system and compiler checks act as static analysis tools that catch errors early in the development process.

T

Thread Safety: A property of code that ensures that it functions correctly during simultaneous execution by multiple threads. Rust's design guarantees thread safety through its ownership and type system, making it a robust choice for concurrent applications.

V

Vulnerability: A weakness in software that can be exploited to compromise its security. Rust's safety guarantees aim to reduce the likelihood of vulnerabilities, making it a reliable language for security-sensitive software development.

W

WebAssembly (Wasm): A binary instruction format designed for safe, fast execution in web browsers. Rust can compile to WebAssembly, allowing developers to create secure applications that run in a browser environment, enhancing web security.

EXPLORATION OF HOW TO USE
RUST TO DEVELOP SECURE TOOLS
AND CRYPTOGRAPHY LIBRARIES.
INCLUDES CONCEPTS SUCH AS
SAFE THREADING AND
VULNERABILITY PREVENTION.

ISBN 9798308269991

9 798308 269991

90000